Faith as Imagination

The Contribution of William F. Lynch, S.J.

Gerald J. Bednar

Lill,

Thanks for all your prayers and support especially during our days at City Hall. Your care and love made the Solicitor's Office a very special place!

Jerry Bednar

Sheed & Ward
Kansas City

1-8-97

Sheed & Ward™ is a service of The National Catholic Reporter
Publishing Company.

Library of Congress Cataloguing-in-Publication Data
Bednar, Gerald J., 1946-
    Faith as imagination : the contribution of William F. Lynch,
S.J. / by Gerald J. Bednar.
       p.   cm.
    Includes bibliographical references and index.
    ISBN 1-55612-907-6 (alk. paper)
    1. Faith—History of doctrines—20th century. 2. Imagination
—Religious aspects—Christianity—History of doctrines—20th
century. 3. Lynch, William F., 1908-1987. I. Title.
BT771.2.B34 1996
230'.2'092—dc21
                           96-46595
                              CIP

Published by: Sheed & Ward
               115 E. Armour Blvd.
               P.O. Box 419492
               Kansas City, MO 64141-6492

To order, call: (800) 333-7373

Contents

With gratitude
to my mother and father,
Angela and Joseph Bednar,
and to the latest additions to the family,
Carolyn Ebner, April 7, 1996,
and
Max Zilvitis, August 24, 1996.

Table of Abbreviations

AAS *Acta Apostolica Sedis*

ASS *Acta Sancta Sedis*

CA William F. Lynch, *Christ and Apollo* (1960).

CP William F. Lynch, *Christ and Prometheus* (1970).

DS H. Denzinger and A. Schönmetzer, *Enchiridion Symbolorum*, ed. 32 (1963).

IF William F. Lynch, *Images of Faith* (1973).

IH William F. Lynch, *Images of Hope* (1965).

IM William F. Lynch, *The Integrating Mind* (1962).

IT Paul Ricoeur, *Interpretation Theory* (1976).

PF Carlos Cirne-Lima, *Personal Faith* (1965).

PP William Lynch, *An Approach to the Metaphysics of Plato Through the Parmenides* (1959).

ST St. Thomas Aquinas, *Summa Theologiae*.

Foreword

THE PURPOSE OF THIS BOOK IS TO EXPLORE FAITH AS IMAGINATION through the challenging and rewarding thought of William F. Lynch, S.J. Many theologians have contributed to the understanding of faith in significant ways by their treatment of faith as belief, as trust, as personal relationship, as dialectical relationship, as praxis and so forth.[1] Yet few aside from William Lynch have elaborated to any great extent on faith as a type of imagination.[2] Lynch is relatively unknown in theological circles, and his thought, therefore, has not had the impact it should.

Although Lynch's writings are always rewarding, they can make for difficult reading. His background in Greek classics and literary criticism quickly becomes evident in his many allusions to dramas and literary critics who are not always familiar to

---

1. See Avery Dulles, *The Assurance of Things Hoped For: A Theology of Christian Faith* (New York: Oxford University Press, 1994) for a masterful treatment of the history of the theology of faith and its models; and his *Models of Revelation* (Garden City, NY: Doubleday, 1983), 246-64.

2. The few who developed their theology in that direction would include the likes of John Henry Newman. See David Hammond, "Imagination in Newman's Phenomenology of Cognition," *Heythrop Journal* 29, no. 1 (1988) and John Coulson, *Religion and Imagination: "In Aid of a Grammar of Assent"* (Oxford: Clarendon, 1981), 46. Pierre Rousellot, whose "Les yeux de la foix," *Recherches de science religieuse* 1 (1910): 242-59; 444-75, highlights our ability to fashion a coherent story from the images given to us; and Hans Urs von Balthasar, who stressed the aesthetic dimension of faith. See, for example, his *The Glory of the Lord: A Theological Aesthetics: Seeing the Form* (New York: Crossroad, 1982), 151 and *Theo-Drama: Theological Dramatic Theory: Prolegomena* (New York: Crossroad, 1983), 125.

theologians. This volume attempts to bring together Lynch's thought on faith as imagination in a systematic way so that his works will be more accessible to the theological community. Certainly faith as imagination is not the only insight that offers an entrée to his writings, but it seems to be one point where his work is particularly promising but neglected.

This work consists of an introduction and four chapters. Each chapter is introduced and concluded with an image from American literature in an effort to illustrate the method that Lynch called "the composition of place." Hopefully, the images will assist in unfolding new aspects of the topic under discussion in each chapter. The Introduction gives background material on Lynch's life and struggles which profoundly affected his writing. Chapter One situates the discussion of the theology of faith as it developed from the latter part of the 19th century, through the Modernist crisis, to the middle of the 20th century when Lynch began publishing his more important articles. Readers who are already familiar with the history of the theology of faith may want to proceed directly from the Introduction to the second chapter. In Chapter Two, the focus shifts to the methodological approaches employed by Lynch. Both his metaphysics and epistemology were profoundly shaped by his understanding of analogy and imagination. The analogical imagination forms the backbone of his method. Chapter Three undertakes a study of Lynch's theology of faith as imagination. Although some people at first tend to view faith as imagination with some skepticism, Lynch constantly reminds his readers that the task of the imagination is to imagine the real. Faith as imagination, in other words, is a way of approaching the reality of God in the midst of this finite world. Faith puts believers in touch with reality through its ironic Christic images. Chapter Four concludes the study with an attempt to draw some implications from Lynch's theology. If faith is accepted as imagination, it should have theological and pastoral implications. The conclusion is meant to stimulate thought so that theologians might appropriate Lynch's approach in their own ways and in their own fields. Finally, a bibliography of Lynch's works is provided for those who want to consult the primary sources.

I would like to thank the people of the Diocese of Cleveland whose generous contributions have made this study possible. This book took its first form as a dissertation for a doctorate in contemporary systematics that I obtained from Fordham University in response to the bishop's request to prepare myself to teach at St. Mary Seminary and Graduate School of Theology. I owe a debt of gratitude to all those at the seminary whose environment provided me with the equipment, material, supplies and the good humor that is needed to go forward with a project like this. I am grateful also to the people of St. Benedict Parish whose hospitality I enjoyed while working on this project in the Bronx.

Special thanks go to John Heaney, professor emeritus at Fordham University, for suggesting this topic to me and offering many helpful suggestions along the way, and to William V. Dych, S.J., professor of theology at Fordham, who first introduced me to William Lynch's works several years before I started doctoral studies. Both have given me very valuable insights in handling Lynch's thought. I would like to thank John Kane, professor of religious studies at Regis University, who is currently developing a work on William Lynch as a social critic. It has been a delight to be able to discuss various issues with a theologian who is so deeply in tune with Lynch's thought. Stephen Babos, S.J., Al Hennelly, S.J., and Richard Viladesau have all seen this book in its early stages and have made very helpful comments. I am also indebted to Michael Pennock and Don Cozzens who offered their insights and encouragement. Joan Nuth, Mary Kay Oosdyke, O.P., David Mason, and Mark Latcovich have read chapters two and three, and have given me very helpful suggestions. To the extent that I have interpreted their comments correctly, this is a much better work.

Of course, I bear responsibility for any shortcomings that surface in the days to come. I can only hope that any of my miscues do not detract from the attention that should be given to William Lynch's theology.

Gerald J. Bednar
St. Mary Seminary and Graduate School of Theology
Diocese of Cleveland

Introduction

THE AMERICAN HISTORIAN DANIEL BOORSTIN ATTESTS TO THE POWER
of the theological imagination through a study of ancient maps.
He reports that by the first century Ptolemy had not only followed
the ancient custom of representing the earth as a sphere, but he
also meticulously charted coastlands and established a grid system
to afford a common reference for the ready location of various
places. How is it that such discoveries and innovations needed to
be rediscovered centuries later?

Boorstin explains that Christian dogma began to impose
"figments of theological imagination on the map of the world."
Consequently, cartographers began to situate Jerusalem in the
middle of their maps, Eden in various places throughout the Atlantic
Ocean, and Gog and Magog in the dark corners of the earth where
devils might someday be expected to appear (according to Rev.
20:8). Thanks to Cosmas of Alexandria, the map of the world
eventually became patterned after the table standing in the Taber-
nacle as was supposedly suggested in the Bible (Heb. 9:1-3). The
world was imagined to be rectangular, flat and symmetrical to
accord with that description. A flat earth would also help Christians
to avoid numerous possible heresies that could be implied from a
rather convoluted theory of people who, if they lived on the other
side of a spherical world, would have to grow downwards in a
region where rain fell upwards. These so-called "Antipodes" would
have to live so opposite to us that questions about the universality
of salvation made a spherical earth unthinkable.[1]

A theological imagination that forgets its proper realm can wreak havoc on the world. It can truly limit our ability to move as the free and rational creatures we were meant to be. While many are aware of the damage that can be inflicted by an unhealthy imagination, few have considered the positive and necessary role that a healthy imagination plays. Any cartographer needs a healthy imagination to be able to compress vast continents onto a single sheet of paper. The endeavor stands or falls on the images that are produced. If the map is successful, the geographical relations among peoples can be assessed with a glance of the eye.

However, those physical relations are only one type of relationship for which people need guidance. External relationships can be traced with relative ease compared to the complex internal world of faith, hope, and love in which people find themselves situated. For those internal realms, we need someone to map the deeper aspects of the relations between people, and between them and their God. These map makers need to assess a different kind of expanse and depth. They need to explore regions of faith that tell us of the presence of the unseen, and assure us of its meaning. What is charted is nothing less than the experience of human living and loving in the face of the divine. Again the imagination is critical to the endeavor. Just as the cartographer's effort will stand or fall on the basis of his images, so will the theologian succeed or fail on the basis of the images that are presented as pathways to the divine.

I. The Career of William F. Lynch, S.J.

In our exploration of the world of faith, we will follow the maps provided by an American Jesuit theological explorer, Fr. William F. Lynch, S.J. His work concerning the role of imagination in faith and theology is truly pioneering. Theologian Ray Hart has written that Lynch, "has homesteaded the land that must be cleared; he has opened a path into the tangled growth of 'theology of the

---

1. Daniel Boorstin, *The Discoverers* (New York: Random House, 1983), 103-104, 107-109.

imagination'."[2] Lynch considered the healthy operation of the imagination as a necessity for accurate theological reflection and as the very center of faith. Of course, the consideration of faith as imagination is only one of several possible ways to consider faith. But it is a promising and fruitful way if it is handled in accord with the various guidelines Lynch describes in his method.

Lynch was uniquely qualified to pursue the development of faith as imagination. William F. Lynch was born in New York City on June 16, 1908, of Michael J. and Mary Maloney Lynch. He was educated at Fordham University and received his Bachelor of Arts degree from the College of Arts and Sciences in 1930.[3] Having earned a Master's degree in Greek philosophy in 1939, that same year Lynch began to publish articles touching on the relationship between poetry and faith.[4] By 1942, he began to refer explicitly to the "Catholic imagination" and its potential to revive modern drama.[5] The next year, he published an article on the reciprocal relationship between liturgy and theater by exploring the power of drama to revive faith.[6] Lynch completed his doctorate in classics in 1943. His dissertation entitled "The Central Problem in Aeschylus' 'Eumenides' " concerned the third play in the Oresteian trilogy, a topic that would later occupy his attention when explaining faith's dramatic march through the finite action of this life, its suffering, and one's eventual passage to new insight.

In 1949, Princeton University recognized Fr. Lynch's scholarly talents by awarding him a fellowship. He remained there until 1950 when he was recalled to Fordham to succeed Fr. Gerald Walsh, S.J., as editor of the Fordham University quarterly,

2. Ray Hart, *Unfinished Man and the Imagination: Toward an Ontology and a Rhetoric of Revelation* (New York: Seabury, 1968), 247 n. 110.

3. I am grateful to the archivist at Fordham University for graciously making available to me the Lynch archives from which much of the following information was obtained.

4. William F. Lynch, "Of Rhythm and Its End," *Spirit: A Magazine of Poetry* 6, no. 5 (November 1939): 150-51; and "The Value of the Arts as Inspirer of Poet and Saint," *America* 62 (December 30, 1939): 327-28.

5. William F. Lynch, "Can the Church Revive the Drama?" *America* 67 (August 29, 1942): 577-78.

6. William F. Lynch, "Liturgy and Theatre," *Liturgical Arts* 12 (November 1943): 3-10.

Thought. It was at this point that Lynch began to develop more fully his views on the need for an imagination that not only discovers but also creates analogies as they can be applied to theological concerns.[7] Fr. Lynch also taught philosophy at Fordham's Graduate School at the time when he published in *Thought* a series of articles specifically focusing on theology and the analogical imagination.[8]

Lynch remained as editor of *Thought* until 1956 when he began to suffer emotional illness through what one reporter called a "harrowing personal experience of severe mental breakdown."[9] His healing process began with his transfer to Georgetown University in 1956. The insights from his ordeal and recovery were later collected in his book, *Images of Hope: Imagination as Healer of the Hopeless* (1965). Psychologists Rollo May and Leslie Farber have hailed this work as an important modern contribution on the significance of the imagination and its relation to our ability to wish.[10] From 1957 to 1962, Lynch taught English at Georgetown and directed the honors program. This period was an unusually productive time in Lynch's literary career, seeing the publication of some of his most important books: *An Approach to the Metaphysics of Plato Through the Parmenides* (1959); *The Image Industries (1959); Christ and Apollo: The Dimensions of the Literary Imagination* (1960); and *The Integrating Mind: An Exploration into Western Thought* (1962).

In 1963, Lynch was assigned as writer in residence at St. Peter's College, Jersey City, New Jersey, where he resided until

---

7. William F. Lynch, "Culture and Belief," *Thought* 25 (September 1950): 463.

8. William F. Lynch, "Theology and the Imagination," *Thought* 29 (Spring 1954): 61-86; "Theology and the Imagination II: The Evocative Symbol," *Thought* 29 (December 1954): 529-54; "Theology and the Imagination III: The Problem of Comedy," *Thought* 30 (Spring 1955): 18-36; and "The Imagination and the Finite," *Thought* 33 (Summer 1958): 205-28.

9. Peter Steinfels, "An Image of Hope," *Commonweal* 114, no. 2, (January 30, 1987): 37. See also Daniel Berrigan, "Father Lynch Dies, Jesuit in the Grand Manner," *National Catholic Reporter* 23, no. 13 (January 23, 1987): 4.

10. Rollo May, *Love and Will* (New York: Dell Publishing, 1969), 209, 213-14, 221. Leslie Farber, foreword to *Images of Hope: Imagination as Healer of the Hopeless,* by William F. Lynch (Notre Dame: University of Notre Dame Press, 1965), 10.

1976. During that time, he regularly taught theology at Woodstock College, the Jesuit New York provincial theologate. During this period, Lynch produced two more books probing the theology of the imagination: in 1970, *Christ and Prometheus: A New Image of the Secular*, and in 1973, *Images of Faith: An Exploration into the Ironic Imagination*, a book that both consolidates and extends his ideas on faith as imagination. In 1978, Fr. Lynch was assigned as writer in residence at the West Side Jesuit community in Manhattan. In 1984, he became the founding editor of *New York Images*, a publication of an independent New York unit of the National Jesuit Institute of the Arts.

After suffering particularly from arthritis for the last 25 years of his life, Fr. Lynch died of leukemia on January 9, 1987, having three times served as editor for various Jesuit publications[11] and having earned the Thomas More Award for Creative Publishing and the Most Distinguished Catholic Book of the Year award for his *Image Industries* in 1959. He also received the National Catholic Book Award in 1970 for his *Christ and Prometheus*, one of his most challenging studies.

II. Discovering the Contribution of William F. Lynch

When William Lynch was ordained in 1945, the prevailing theology in the Church was cast in terms of Scholasticism. Lynch's Ignatian spirituality, his background in Greek philosophy, and his familiarity with Greek drama prepared him to assess carefully the role of the imagination in the lives of the faithful. But if he was going to remain true to concrete, finite existence, as he constantly maintained that a healthy life of the imagination enables a person to do, he would find himself at odds with two groups of Catholic scholars: literary critics who tended to look for principles and morals to embody in plays, and Scholastic theologians whose system was largely deduced from first principles that were taken

---

11. In 1948, he served for a year as the editor of the *Messenger of the Sacred Heart*, a monthly publication that catered to the popular Catholic devotion of the day. His efforts to coax the publication into a more profound piety failed.

as evident. In both spheres, Lynch would argue for an inductive approach rather than the then favored deductive approach.

In demonstrating the contribution of William Lynch, it will be helpful to review the Scholastic theology of faith in its historical context. Chapter One will set forth the particularly Catholic concerns about faith. The Church was beset by the rationalists who considered faith as inferior to knowledge. Indeed, faith was considered as illusory. The objective, extrinsic approach of the Scholastics will be contrasted against the approach taken by Maurice Blondel's philosophy of action. A rather disparate group of scholars known as "Modernists" developed theological insights deriving from the turn to the subject. Contrary to the Scholastics, Modernists proposed that faith necessarily deals with the subjective dimension of the believer's life, and, therefore, looks for evidence that is intrinsic to that life. Official Church documents dealt harshly with Modernist concerns, and, even as Lynch was developing his insights on the analogical imagination as a necessity for good theology, Pius XII's encyclical, *Humani Generis* (AAS 562), specifically criticized the imagination as a hindrance to sound theological study. Clearly Lynch's theology of faith marked a radical shift from the intellectualist emphasis that was favored in Scholastic theology.

In Chapter Two, we will explore Lynch's method of employing an "analogical imagination" that facilitates rather than hinders the theological effort. Lynch explains that it takes no great effort to imagine the merely fanciful. Unicorns are a dime a dozen. What is needed is the ability to imagine the real. Lynch's guidelines here offer true theological insight in attending to the data of human life and the experience of grace.

In Chapter Three, we will consider faith as imagination. For Lynch, faith is primarily a way of composing reality. It is a way of experiencing human life at its depths. That experience generates and receives images that are both a result of faith and a motivation for deeper faith. Those images are both produced and discovered as a person lives in what Lynch calls the "ironic Christic imagination." It is an imagination that leaves room for the ironic as Christ experienced it. It can see strength in weakness, hope in hopeless circumstances, the infinite in the finite, and life in death. It is an imagination that defeats our temptation to simplify reality by imposing neat, univocal images on the beings we encounter. It rejoices in the imagination's ability to allow God's creatures to show themselves to us so we can form appropriate images.

Finally, the Conclusion will place the contribution of William Lynch in its theological context and will suggest some of the many implications that can be derived from his thought. Clearly Lynch has proposed a paradigm shift in our thought on faith, and his contribution will be viewed in light of those Catholic theologians who follow in the tradition of Pierre Rousselot and Joseph Maréchal who developed the intuitive aspects of Thomism. The thought of Carlos Cirne-Lima, a theologian who attempted to build a bridge between Scholastic and more modern conceptions of faith, will be inspected in an attempt to sharpen our focus on the direction in which Lynch's theology proposes that we move. Lynch's contribution will be considered in the context of what is required of a theologian who attempts to respond to Bernard Lonergan's injunction that one must be attentive in order to be intelligent, rational, and responsible. Lynch's contributions include his insights that see faith as drama, faith as a profound exercise of freedom, and faith as that which offers a person a single sensibility that enables one to live in the midst of the many contrary poles that confront every human being (i.e., the immanent and the transcendent, nature and supernature, reason and faith, etc.).

The images we choose in coping with various issues in life will be decisive in both theology and faith. Images cannot be chosen lightly, for, as Lynch will caution us, they are packed with all sorts of choices and directions that are usually not evident at the outset. People need a reliable mapmaker to guide them through the forest of images that have developed throughout two millennia of Christian prayer and devotion. In choosing Lynch as a guide, we choose one whose sense of direction has the ring of truth and whose understanding of the dramatic element in life is faithful to what people already "know" but have been unable to say for themselves. Through Lynch's theology, we poor explorers are given invaluable aid in purging our maps of the mere "figments of theological imagination" and in charting a true course whose landmarks are more than simply illusions.

CHAPTER ONE

Faith and Imagination: The Issues

NOT FAR FROM MANHATTAN, THERE LIES A HAUNTED COVE CALLED Sleepy Hollow. It was there that the problem of faith was put in legendary form for Americans by Washington Irving. He told us of the trials of Ichabod Crane. By day, in his schoolhouse, he was rational, shrewd, and ruthless. By night, among the common folk, he was credulous, affable, and downright gullible – especially when it came to tales of the supernatural.

One night, what Ichabod dreaded seemed to come true in the form of a practical joke as he encountered the famed headless horseman of Sleepy Hollow. In fear, Ichabod spurred his horse toward the bridge where, legend had it, the headless horseman could not follow. As he reached the bridge, Ichabod glanced back just in time to see his pursuer carrying his own head (in fact, a pumpkin). The headless horseman hurled his "head" as a weapon at the frightened Ichabod who, some say, was never heard from again.[1]

Is faith really akin to a practical joke on the gullible? Is the head really severed from the heart and used as a weapon against it? Or is there a place of integration that can give each its due, while receiving from each a valid, reliable contribution to our view of reality? One of the more difficult problems in theology

---

1. Washington Irving, "The Legend of Sleepy Hollow," in *The Sketch Book* (New York: The New American Library of World Literature, 1961), 329-60.

has been the problem of integrating the head and the heart, the natural and the supernatural, the day and the night, in ways that are palatable to modernity. Some theories offer nothing more than a headless horseman. Other theories offer only a ruthless head that is used as a weapon against a credulous heart. Still others juxtapose head and heart in quite artificial ways, as if one were merely holding a pumpkin. This is the monumental problem of faith that has haunted the hollows of theology, especially since the Enlightenment.

Before turning to William Lynch's thought, we will consider Scholasticism, the predominant theology of his day, to see what gave rise to its theory and to the reactions it drew particularly during the Modernist crisis. Since Lynch did not write in conjunction with any particular school of theology, as our survey unfolds, brief references to the concerns that Lynch highlighted will be noted in order to locate Lynch on the theological spectrum. This survey will help place his work in the context of some of the modern issues on faith, and it will help to show how his thought offers a basic shift from Scholastic theories on faith.

I. The General Context

The challenge of the Enlightenment created a crisis for theologians. The element that made Galileo's case so complex, the element of faith (that seemed to assure us that man was at the center of the universe) was unnecessary to consider as long as one presented reasons that were sufficient to explain the phenomena under question. One need not appeal to the mysteries of God to handle problems that the rules of evidence and a little bit of shrewd investigation could solve.

Not only science but also history could eventually be treated without reference to the transcendent. No one had thought of scriptural stories as "mythical" prior to the rationalist approach. It was simply the language through which the faithful had been able to perceive and communicate the presence of the divine in this world. However, symbols of the presence of the transcendent in history were now summoned before the bar of reason and were found to be "irrational." For Voltaire, faith sinks far below the level of rational belief. Faith is simply obedience, credulity in the face of the incredible.[2]

With this critique of faith and sacred history, the stage was set for those who would offer a totally immanent view of history. Without a transcendent goal assured by faith, history must find its meaning in the immanent. The eschatological dimension of faith became immanentized through the thinking of such men as the French economist Turgot, who served as Louis XVI's finance minister. He solved the problem of meaning by searching within history for "lines of meaning," such as the continuing trend toward intensified commerce. But these immanent lines of meaning could have significance only for humankind in general. The concrete individual was lost from view.[3]

That immanentizing trend was eventually accompanied by the chaos of the French Revolution. The union of altar and throne, a symbol of grace and nature, was destroyed in France. The principle of order in society seemed no longer as reliable as reason, but as whimsical as the will. The first half of the nineteenth century was thus largely taken up with efforts to restore the order of the *ancien régime*.

Those like Louis de Bonald and Joseph de Maistre, who were dissatisfied with the new trend toward secularism, could engage in a traditionalism that searched for the truth of order by discerning "what mankind had always believed." Others, such as Michael Bakunin and Karl Marx, looked instead to the future for an ordering principle, since they considered the vestiges of the past to be precisely the problem. Only in the future could a truly human history begin. In the meantime, the precepts of faith

---

2. "What is faith? Is it to believe that which is evident? No. It is perfectly evident to my mind that there exists a necessary, eternal, supreme, and intelligent being. This is no matter of faith, but of reason. . . . Faith consists in believing not what seems true, but what seems false to our understanding. . . . It can be nothing but the annihilation of reason . . . [I]t is clear that if my *reason* is not persuaded, *I* am not persuaded." M. de Voltaire, *A Philosophical Dictionary*, vol. I, (London: W. Dugdale, 1843), 473-74.

3. Eric Voegelin, *From Enlightenment to Revolution* (Durham: Duke University Press, 1975), 21, 94-95.

constituted only so many "imaginary flowers" that adorned the chains of the workers.

Despite such disorder, Pius IX attempted to search for some sort of accommodation with liberal ideas early in his pontificate. In 1848, the year of revolutions, Pius IX's prime minister, Pelegrino Rossi, was murdered and the Papal residence was threatened by rioting. Once again the papacy was forced into exile. The Pope's return in 1850 by virtue of the French Army marked the beginning of the Pope's status as the "prisoner" of the Vatican. The Church's turn towards a monarchized, ultramontane, centralized self-governance needs to be seen in the context of such turmoil. Pius IX's earlier openness to liberalism proved in his eyes to be a vain effort to trust in a fallen human nature.

During this period, Catholic theology was perceived as being in a state of disarray. The French Revolution and the Napoleonic wars had left French seminary libraries and faculties in shambles. Eclectic approaches in philosophy were commonplace. De Bonald offered his traditionalism, while Louis Bautain elaborated theories promoting a fideism that asserted an unprovable basis for all knowledge, including our knowledge of God. Georg Hermes attempted to base his theology on practical reason in order to respond to modern Kantian insights on the nature of faith. The German Idealists of the Catholic Tübingen School tried to explain the dynamic of faith in terms of the idea of the Kingdom of God that continuously unfolds in history. If some thought German Idealism tended to pantheism, Anton Günther's dualism reached for the opposite extreme in insisting on the separation of the divine and the human, and of the spirit and the body. Many thought his system fell into rationalism. Contrary to Günther, the ontologists claimed that God can be experienced as a constitutive "part" of every finite thing a person perceives. The experience of knowing and loving, according to them, yields a direct experience of God.

By mid-nineteenth century, there was such a welter of theological opinion that one would be hard pressed to describe a common position on faith. Most systems were generated in response to the challenges of rationalism that not only had denied the objectivity of the act of supernatural faith but also had begun to replace the "substance of things hoped for" with an entirely immanent faith in humankind.

Viewing itself as a source of order, the papacy intervened continuously from 1846 to 1866 to condemn ontologism (DS 2841-2847), pantheism (DS 2901), traditionalism (DS2812-2813), dualism (DS 2833), naturalism (DS 2901-2902), socialism (DS 2918), communism (DS 2918), and rationalism (DS 2775; 2903-2914). Clearly, the concern of the Church at this point was not to develop new creative university theologies. Priests needed a common seminary training to enable them to present a clear, unambiguous message to parishioners. The concern was not merely pastoral and dogmatic, but political as well. Bishops, especially in Germany, objected to the state's control over religion and appreciated the value of a strong Rome in helping them protect common believers from state interference in religious education. Italian unification also presented a threat to the Papal States, which were considered necessary for Catholic unity.

II. The Scholastic Reaction

Scholasticism seemed well suited to respond to the Church's needs not only because it was untouched by modern philosophy, but also because its epistemology could appeal to the common person. One need not posit the existence of an "Idea" that somehow lurked "behind" things, giving them direction and order. Nor did one need to attempt to discern innate ideas.

In a bold stroke of epistemological decisiveness, Scholastics simply posited what seemed obvious to everyone: the five senses, as sources of knowledge, must simply be trusted in the area of their competence.[4] Error is only accidental. Since a person is a unity of sense and intellect, discursive reason is not cut off from the world of reality. Reason is capable of metaphysical knowledge, and, in fact, can argue its way to the existence of God on

---

4. G. Van Riet, *Thomistic Epistemology: Studies Concerning the Problem of Cognition in the Contemporary Thomistic School*, trans. G. Franke (St. Louis: B. Herder, 1963), 114ff.

the speculative plane by using abstractive realism. Hence, faith is reasonable, and it can even be shown to be scientific.

Unfortunately, leading Scholastics like Joseph Kleutgen and Matteo Liberatore adopted a modified Suarezian approach to Thomas' work and thus missed some of the profound metaphysics by which Thomas' system could be seen as open to development.[5] Both missed the richer conception of Thomas, who described being as that whose act is existence. Both, therefore, fell into a unitary system that formed the backbone of "integralism," a doctrine that proposed that truth is a divinely guaranteed, unchanging, objective whole that exists outside of the person. Truth, therefore, consists of the mind's conformity to the thing known. Once an adequate idea is formed, any deviation from it can only result in error. "Development of a truth" could occur only in terms of logical inferences or more up-to-date expressions for the same basic concept. Furthermore, if an idea is placed in the mind through the revelation of God and is accepted on faith, à fortiori the believer must hold fast to that piece of information since it has been granted from an infallible source. Real truth fell from heaven and could not be considered as relative or as historical in any sense.[6] Integralism became so rigid that á priori answers even began to dictate the reading of Scripture. The imagination was considered only as a source of error.

In view of such conceptions, Maurice Blondel's approach to truth as an accurate disclosure of the subjective experience of life constituted one of the most disconcerting challenges to the Scholastics. William Lynch will later detect in the proponents of integralism an unhealthy reluctance to grow, as well as an unrealistic attachment to a univocal conception of truth even though they paid lip service to analogy. The analogical quality of truth will form an important element in Lynch's theology, and it

---

5. See Frederick Copleston, *A History of Philosophy III, Ockham to Suarez* (Westminster, Md.: Newman, 1963), 397; Gerald McCool, *From Unity to Pluralism: The Internal Evolution of Thomism* (New York: Fordham University Press, 1989), 31-32; and Etienne Gilson, *Being and Some Philosophers*, 2d ed. (Toronto: Garden City, 1949), 105.

6. Louis Billot, *De Immutabilitate Traditionis contra Modernam Haeresim Evolutionismi* (Rome: Pontificia Universitas Gregoriana, 1919), 47-48, 101.

will help justify consideration of the role that an "analogical imagination" must play.

A. *Dei Filius* and *Aeterni Patris*

By April of 1870, both the political and theological worlds had become so threatening that Pius IX convened the first ecumenical council at the Vatican. The Pope felt it necessary to clarify and consolidate the Church's position on faith. In *Dei Filius*, the Council stated that since faith and reason proceed from a common divine source, they should be viewed as mutually supportive. Indeed, right reason can establish the the existence of God.

Faith, on the other hand, can guard reason from error. Faith was defined as follows:

> The Catholic Church professes truly this faith, which "is the beginning of human salvation," to be truly a super- natural virtue, by which, with the grace of God inspiring and sustaining [us], we believe to be true what is revealed by him, not because of the thing's intrinsic truth per- ceived in the light of natural reason, but because of the authority of the revealing God himself who can neither be deceived nor deceive.[7]

In recognizing the two-fold order of knowledge, reason and revelation, *Dei Filius* tended to oppose nature and grace. In their discussion of what was due to "pure nature," Scholastics tended to juxtapose artificially the supernatural and the natural, and conse- quently to lose sight of the concrete person, just as Turgot had done albeit for different reasons. As we will see, theology's ability to preserve the concrete whole as a unity will be a critical factor for Lynch in determining the success of any theological endeavor.

Of course *Dei Filius* included Scholastic concerns, such as the judgment of credibility that precedes the act of faith. Credi- bility constituted a judgment by the believer that a particular

---

7. Hanc vero fidem, quae "humanae salutis initium est," Ecclesia catholica profitetur, virtutem esse supernaturalem, qua, Dei aspirante et adiuvante gratia, ab eo revelata vera esse credimus, non propter intrinsecam rerum veritatem naturali rationis lumine perspectam, sed propter auctoritatem ipsius Dei revelantis, qui nec falli nec fallere potest (DS 3008).

matter of faith was not only possible, but probable. Jean Bainvel offers the example of one who proposes that the number of stars is an odd number. Such a statement would not be considered credible because there is no basis for affirming or negating the proposition. Any decision without additional facts would be merely arbitrary. Thus, if it is an angel or a scientist who proposes that the number of stars is odd, then one may judge it as a credible statement. In religious faith, the judgment of credibility is founded on such additional facts as miracles and prophecies.[8]

Dei Filius also included the rather un-Scholastic contribution of Cardinal Victor Dechamps, who proposed that the contemporary Church continually furnishes a sign of credibility by the very way it lives the Gospel. If we reflected honestly on the deepest longings of human life, the truth and goodness of the Church would present themselves to us as the authentic promise of fulfillment of those needs through the Christian faith. The "interior facts" of our lives will find the promise of fulfillment in the "exterior fact" of the Church. Thus, Chapter III refers to the Church as a "great and perpetual motive of credibility" ["magnum . . . et perpetuum . . . motivum credibilitatis"] (DS 3013). That so-called "method of Providence" would form a significant resource for Modernists in the years to come.

Two years after the Council, the Italian armies marched on Rome. Leo XIII, as Cardinal Pecci, had been deeply involved in Pius IX's program to rectify the ills of modernity. Despite the strong support given to the papacy by Vatican I, the Pope was increasingly isolated from other world leaders. Protestant leadership had established itself in Berlin, England, and America. The Pope could look only to the common people for support. A truly universal theology based on a perennial philosophy was needed.

Leo promoted the restoration of Scholasticism through the encyclical *Aeterni Patris,* in hopes of finding that objective immutable order which could be proven to all and could therefore serve as a basis for a common understanding in a Church still plagued by eclecticism. It had already established a foothold in Italy and

---

8. J. V. Bainvel, *Faith and the Act of Faith*, trans. L. Sterck (New York: B. Herder, 1926), 95, 102.

Germany, although its adherents were not generally held in high esteem by university theologians. Scholastic philosophy lauded itself on being the handmaid of theology – highly objective, scientific, based on evidence, logically ordered, subservient to proper authority, universal, timeless, free of modern culture, and ahistorical.

Those who favored the Scholastic revival quickly stepped up the pace of reform. Faculties, especially in seminaries, were shuffled to reflect the desires of the encyclical. Although Cardinal Mercier sought out the original text of Thomas, most Scholastics were unaware of the diversity that existed within the various Thomistic schools. While some sensed the need to return to the original texts, others felt the need to train priests who could give the laity clear and coherent guidance during those troubled times. Manuals were thus produced to offer a system that would save priests from a confusing eclecticism. Unfortunately, in their zeal to fulfill the ideals of *Aeterni Patris* and to remain within the confines of officially approved theology, the manualists missed the subtleties of Thomas' thought.

Consequently, the system appeared rationalistic, impersonal, conceptual, deductive and discursive. The intuitive, an important element for Thomistic epistemology, was given scant attention. Nevertheless, the system seemed to offer answers at a time when questions were beginning to shake the very foundations of the Church. Although the appearance of manuals is understandable, their mediocrity was marked with a philosophy that too frequently begged the question on the basis of á prioris, definitions, and presumably timeless Latin formulas.

B. Ongoing Threats to Scholasticism

As the Scholastics attempted to order the intellectual world of faith and reason, the political world reflected analogous struggles between the sacred and the secular. Bismarck's *Kulturkampf*, the "May Laws" of 1872, the suppression of the Jesuits, and state control of religious education posed thorny problems that were eventually settled through a concordat. However, such solutions posed problems of their own because they appeared to place

Church leadership once again in league with the ruling classes who might easily use religion as the opium of the masses.

Other threats to the faith were not so subtle. Charles Darwin offered a plausible hypothesis on the development of humans that did not require any special divine intervention. Friederich Nietzsche claimed that life is "will to power," an expression of a person's passional nature. Faith is nothing more than an instinct, a cowardly retreat from the facts.[9] Indeed, his god is not Apollo whose introspective musings and measured theories of self-restraint stymie any action, but the wild Dionysus who is given to a life of ecstasy.[10] For Nietzsche, life is either lived in the context of the finite, which man disdains, or in the context of the infinite, an illusion that titillates the imagination. Love of heaven necessitates the hatred of the earth, and spawns an unnatural desensualization. Religion has killed the human, now it must kill God.[11]

Others began to consider faith according to wholly new sciences. By the turn of the century, Max Weber would view faith in the light of sociology. William James considered the act of faith strictly in its psychological setting. Sigmund Freud would later expose faith to the harsh light of his psychoanalytic method and would conclude that it is merely an elaborate neurotic attempt to avoid an encounter with reality. Further challenges came from scholars like Ernst Troeltsch who began a comparative study of religion that showed alarming similarities between pagan religions and Christianity.

In spite of the Scholastic synthesis, in spite of the many papal warnings that had been issued over the years, and in spite of Vatican I, the old challenges to the value and significance of faith only intensified. Increasingly, Catholic theologians felt the pressure to refine the theology of faith. Those challenges were not lost on Lynch. As we will see, he responded especially to the Nietzschean attack in precisely the terms of Apollo and Dionysus.

---

9. Friederich Nietzsche, *Beyond Good and Evil* (Chicago: Henry Regnery, 1955) 15, 20, 98-99.

10. Friederich Nietzsche, *The Birth of Tragedy,* in *The Birth of Tragedy and The Case of Wagner,* trans. W. Kaufmann (New York: Random House, 1967), § 1, 2, 7; *Beyond Good and Evil,* 235.

11. Nietzsche, *Beyond Good and Evil,* 61-62, 70-71, 150.

The Freudian attacks also attracted Lynch's attention in terms of Christian hope and one's ability to wish.

C. Faith in Scholastic Thought

In response to the crisis posed by the rationalists, Scholastic theologians fashioned a rather tight system to defend the legitimacy of the act of faith in terms of reason itself. Roger Aubert has identified three Scholastic lines of thought on faith that had developed by the turn of the century. They were the dominant position, the position of Billot and Bainvel, and the Dominican position.[12]

i. The Dominant Position. The dominant Scholastic position on faith can be found in the works of G. Perrone, J. Kleutgen, J. Franzelin, J. Sheeben, and others. Faith was viewed by them in terms of propositional truths that were accepted on the authority of another. In analyzing the steps involved in the act of faith, it was shown that one is presented with certain "evidences" of what is to be believed. Then a judgment of credibility is made. This judgment determines the probability of the proposed belief. Some grounds are needed to convince a reasonable person to believe the proposition. Otherwise, belief would be arbitrary.[13]

Of course a person could be prejudiced against the faith right from the start. A *pius credulitatis affectus*, a pious feeling inclining the person to believe, or a certain openness to believe, was considered necessary. Grace plays its role in bringing the person to the point where the judgment of credibility can be made. If the person makes the judgment of credibility and is open to the faith, he or she may then believe the testimony. At that point, a judgment of credentity is made. Credentity implies that the proposition is not only credible but is also true. The person has an obligation to believe, once the intellect recognizes the truth of the proposition. The will is then authorized to command

---

12. Roger Aubert, *Le Problème de l'acte de foi*, 2d ed. (Louvain: Warny 1950), 226ff.

13. J. Perrone, *Praelectiones Theologicae de Virtutibus Fidei, Spei et Caritas* (Ratisbonae: Sumptibus, Chartis et Typis Frederici Pustet, 1865), 226-27, 254-55, 2.

the assent of the intellect. Of course, this analysis allowed for the anomalous possibility of a person who might make the judgment of credentity and might willfully refuse to believe. Such a possiblity was thought necessary to preserve the freedom of faith.[14]

In order to locate faith in the realm of objective truth, a syllogism was employed. What God says is true; God has revealed this proposition; therefore, it is true. The extrinsic evidence, the testimony of Scripture and Tradition, and the intrinsic evidence of reason could discursively lead a person to make the act of faith. The faith of the dominant Scholastic school needed to be rational and objective. If it were only subjective, as Cardinal Mercier quipped, it would be like trying to hang a painting of a picture on the painting of a hook.[15]

Although Scholastics met the rationalists on their own grounds in establishing that faith is reasonable, the approach caused problems. The role of grace, for example, remained unclear. Grace "helped" a person make the judgment of credibility, but the help seemed unnecessary and totally extrinsic to the process. It almost seemed to be an excuse to make faith meritorious. Indeed, the entire argument was presented as rationally compelling for those who were reasonably intelligent and were not prejudiced.

ii. Billot and Bainvel. Louis Billot and Jean Bainvel reacted against a "faith" that seemed to be the conclusion of a syllogism. Their system presented supernatural faith as having a psychological structure that is no different from natural faith. Faith is simply belief in the testimony of another.

Those who believe through a "scientific faith" inspect closely the witness and testimony they are given. After verifying the sources in the manner of a judge or a historian, the person may set aside all doubts and decide to believe. Scientific faith uses the following syllogism: (1) a statement duly guaranteed is true; (2) this statement is duly guaranteed; (3) therefore, it is true.[16]

---

14. Perrone, *Praelectiones Theologicae*, 254-55, 267-69, 292, 272. Camillus Mazzella, *De Virtutibus Infusis* (Neapoli: Pontificia M. D'Auria, 1908), 824, 849. Aubert, *Le Problème*, 229.

15. Aubert, *Le Problème*, 235, 238.

Faith based on simple authority, on the other hand, occurs when a person dispenses with preliminary investigations and simply decides to believe solely on the authority of the witness. Bainvel likened it to the child who willingly believes a proposition simply because mother said it. This type of faith involves a homage, a sacrifice, an act of the will to submit oneself to the testimony of another. It is no longer a question of evidence and credibility; it is a question of one's relationship of submission to the one who testifies.[17]

Bainvel recognized that the certitude of faith presupposes the fact of revelation. God simply graces most people with an interior illumination by which they accept the fact of revelation. They may be led to it by the word of their mothers, teachers, priests, or others. Other fortunate people such as Lazarus, the Apostles, and various saints throughout the ages, receive direct revelations that result in their certitude. Still others may attain certitude of the fact of revelation by the use of their reason. The Catholic faith could be scientifically demonstrated as the faith that contains the deposit of revelation. An infallible witness must be believed. Since the infallibility of the witness could be presumed, the truth of the revealed propositions was considered assured. C. Pesch claimed such reasoning was completely legitimate in the process of making the judgments of credibility and credentity, but not the act of faith itself.[18]

True faith occurs only when the "yes" of faith proceeds solely on the basis of the word of God – not on any preliminary investigations, no matter how compelling they may be.[19] If one is

---

16. J. V. Bainvel, *Faith*, 16.

17. Ibid., 13, 38-39, 48. Although the example of the child who puts faith in the mother seems persuasive at first glance, one might question whether children believe because mother said it or because mother was clever enough to motivate her child to *want* to believe it. What child is going to believe a mother who says there is no Santa Claus? Parents also find it difficult to make their children believe that an all-chocolate diet will be less satisfying than one that is nutritionally balanced.

18. Bainvel, *Faith*, 69-71, 73. Christianus Pesch, *Compendium Theologiae Dogmaticae*, Vol. III (Friburg: Herder, 1924), 248.

19. Bainvel, *Faith*, 80-81. Billot and Bainvel diverge in their thought concerning the supernatural quality of the formal object of faith. Billot proposed, ". . .

convinced by a syllogism that God has revealed something, the true believer must set aside that knowledge and make an act of the will to believe simply on the basis of the authority of God. The will does not make up for insufficient motives, but it declares which motive will be the ultimate ground of belief. Thus, the will sets the intellect on its search, conquers the vain products of the imagination, and senses the attractiveness of truth. The intellect attains certainty concerning the fact of revelation, exhibits the advantages of faith to the will, and intimates the obligation to believe. Hence, in answer to rationalist critics, Bainvel could claim that the content of faith is rationally certain. In answer to the fideist critics, it can be shown that the content of the faith is transformed into religious belief only when it is believed because God said it.

Billot and Bainvel's analysis of faith relied too heavily on a univocal concept of faith based on extrinsic testimony. Faith for them constituted belief in the experience of another person quite apart from the experience of the believer. Articles of faith could be wholly extrinsic to the believer's life, yet they were to be held with certitude. The issue of credibility therefore was considered as a condition wholly extrinsic to a person's life. Daly notes that Billot employed an á priori agnosticism concerning the nature and content of revelation. God could have said anything. Billot at the same time relied on a sort of á posteriori fideism in his consideration of evidences. Miracles and prophecies assume magnified proportions because they back up the content of revelation and need not have anything whatever to do with human life.[20] The religious aspect of faith seems to be composed of miracles and prophecies instead of the transformed existence that a believer attains with faith. As we will see, Lynch will take

---

quod fides supernaturalis formali objecto non differt a fide quae naturae viribus eliceretur" ["that faith by the supernatural formal object does not differ from faith which is elicited by natural powers"]. L. Billot, *De Ecclesia Christi* (Rome: Libraria Giachetti, Filii et Soc., 1909), 37. Bainvel clearly taught that the supernatural light differs from the natural powers of reason, although he was admittedly quite vague in explaining precisely how they differed. See Bainvel, *Faith*, 142.

20. Gabriel Daly, *Transcendence and Immanence: A Study in Catholic Modernism and Integralism* (Oxford: Clarendon, 1980), 17.

issue with such extrinsic conceptions by his recognition of faith's activity in the core of the believer.

iii. The Dominican School. The third development within Scholasticism was proposed largely through the work of scholars such as A. Gardeil, M. Schwalm, and E. Hugon writing in the Dominican school. Their leading insight drew attention to the role of grace.

The issue of grace must be decisive in the act of religious faith. Departing from Billot and Bainvel, the Dominican Thomists rejected the theory that the act of religious faith strictly parallels the act of natural faith. The difference lies in the supernatural formal object of faith. When people are graced with religious faith, divine action is perceptible. They are seized by a new way of seeing things. While they do not "see" God, they know they have been touched by the divine. The will, at that point, not only sets aside imprudent doubts but also directs the intelligence to the divine.

According to T. Pègues, the full religious act of faith cannot consist merely in the intellectual conviction that certain propositions are true. After all, even the demons could attain such dead faith. Nor could the act of faith proceed from just any movement of the will. Religious faith results from a free decision "oriented in a certain way, by a certain affective movement, towards the truth proposed in the name of God."[21] Such theories need to be advanced with great care because any mention of the affective dimension by which the faithful are lured to the divine may become confused with the sentimentality and subjectivism associated with Schleiermacher, Kant, and the Modernists.

The Dominican Thomists had sensed a major difficulty. The mystery of faith could be known only in a mysterious way, that must nevertheless still be rational. The supernatural light of faith was given a place in the act of faith, but the role of the will still appeared to be extrinsic to the act. It seemed arbitrary. The concern to hold fast to the objective validity of the knowledge given in faith produced a suspicion of the will. After all, one could not simply will something to be true. For the Dominican School, revelation was considered in two ways: supernatural in the way it comes (e.g.:

---

21. Thomas Pègues, "Chronique de théologie morale spéculative," *Revue thomiste* 20 (1912): 360.

through miracles and prophecies) which is susceptible to reason; and supernatural in its substance which is not attainable by reason, but only by the light of faith. Hence, revelation is reasonable, but not attainable by natural knowledge.[22]

Progress was clearly being achieved within the Scholastic ranks, but that progress was prodded, pushed and shaped by new discoveries and theories that were proposed by the modern world. The painful days of the Modernist crisis would strike right at the heart of the Scholastic program.

D. John Henry Newman

The thought of John Henry Newman (1801-1890) was important not only because it formed one of the more significant resources for the Modernist thinkers but also because it constituted a significant theology in its own right. Newman saw the relationship between faith and reason in more personal terms than his Scholastic contemporaries, yet he also seemed to be more careful than the Modernists in the way in which he conceived and expressed that relationship. His theological synthesis was so impressive to Lynch that he included him along with Plato and St. Ignatius as one of his "great abiding friends."[23]

Newman contended that the term "reason" must be considered in various ways. One way, à posteriori reasoning, relies on evidences. Another way, logical reasoning, relies on principles of analysis. There is also a reasoning process about religion that

---

22. Aubert, *Le Problème*, 262.

23. Mary Jo Weaver, *Newman and the Modernists* (New York: University Press of America, 1985). William Lynch, *Christ and Apollo: The Dimensions of the Literary Imagination* (Notre Dame: University of Notre Dame Press, 1960), xiv. Newman also appeared to be more flexible than some of the Modernists. For example, in 1847, the year after his conversion, he found it possible to endorse a set of Scholastic principles on faith while still adhering to very different principles that he had set forth in his Oxford University sermons. Newman again endorsed the set of Scholastic principles on faith in 1877, seven years after writing his *Grammar of Assent*. He was capable of holding a position while at the same time admitting the validity of a system very different from his own. See John Henry Newman, "Theses de Fide," in "Cardinal Newman's Theses de Fide and His Proposed Introduction to the French Translation of the University Sermons," ed. H. Tristram, *Gregorianum* 18 (1937): 226-41.

gropes for its way without the light of faith. None of those ways can furnish the light of faith. However, there is a type of reasoning that is based on á prioris which include the light of faith. Hence, that reasoning process is wholly consistent with faith. Indeed, it is part of faith. It is the intellectual probing of which Thomas wrote. One cannot attain faith through reason, but once a person becomes a believer, reason becomes part of faith's very life.[24]

Newman claimed that faith involves an assent to convergent or antecedent probabilities. An Englishman may be convinced that Great Britain is an island, but he may become flustered if asked for logical proof. Nevertheless, he will continue to adhere to that position with certitude. Newman claimed that such certitude is justified by "informal inference" from a complex set of facts, all of which converge on a person's judgment of a concrete situation. Syllogism has practically no part to play in such a process.[25]

The activity of grace within each believer moves a person to faith. That grace gives the light of faith by which the person can see how all the antecedent probabilities fit together to speak the message of the Gospels. Believers are graced with that moment of insight that reveals the "whole" that, just moments before, consisted of only so many disparate parts. It is like the lawyer who finally sees how the facts fit together to make a case. Serious believers have a faith that is "more personal" than that which can be attained only from external evidences of miracles. There is a sort of instinct for the faith that is built from the anticipations and presumptions of the mind itself. God is addressed as a person and not as a doctrine. This type of faith then becomes a principle of action.[26]

Epistemologically, imagination for Newman is necessary for real apprehension, which grasps a proposition as an image, and for notional apprehension, in which the imagination abstracts from the whole to allow a person to focus on one aspect of that whole.[27] Mere notional apprehension can be misleading, how-

24. John Henry Newman, *Sermons before the University of Oxford* (London: Francis & John Rivington, 1844), xi-xvii; *A Reason for the Hope Within: Sermons on the Theory of Religious Belief* (Denville: Dimension Books, 1985), 195, 199.

25. John Henry Newman, *An Essay in Aid of a Grammar of Assent* (Notre Dame: University of Notre Dame Press, 1979), 234, 158, 149, 162-63.

26. Ibid., 291; Newman, *A Reason for the Hope*, 219, 179.

ever, especially as notions are inferred from other notions because the imagination has not been used to keep the whole
together, but to dissect it, leaving us with a part that never
subsisted on its own.

The illative sense, on the other hand, results in an "enlargement" of thought, a constantly recurring theme in Lynch's theology.
This enlargement of thought seeks the higher viewpoint. It allows
the lawyer to see a story in the facts that are otherwise disconnected.
Under the influence of the illative sense, data become clues that
tell a story. A prophet, in the moment of inspiration, sees in an
event the key that reconciles what was heretofore a confusing
history. The imagination's grasp of the whole enables one to come
to the point of real assent. Many, for example, admitted the iniquity
of slavery notionally. But it was not until an "organized agitation"
affected people's imagination that something was done to abolish
it. The imagination not only gives an image of the whole, it enables
assent and spurs people to action.[28]

Faith comes, it seems, as an enlargement of the mind, not by
adding facts, but by a "change of place" that gives a "connected
view" or a new "insight into the bearing and influence of each part
on every other." It is a "living knowledge" of "mutual relations."
The one that lacks the faithful imagination is like the sailor who
visits many ports but never succeeds in understanding how one
port relates geographically to another. He views the tapestry, as it
were, from the wrong side. Faith may be considered, in Newman's
thought, as the grace whereby a person changes position, or
converts, to view the correct side of the tapestry, the artful side that
brings the threads together in a new and meaningful fashion.[29]

If the central problem of faith was found in the struggle to
keep together contraries such as the natural and the supernatural,
the immanent and transcendent, etc., and to view things in their
connectedness to one another, then perhaps the imagination

---

27. See David Hammond, "Imagination in Newman's Phenomenology of
Cognition," *Heythrop Journal* 29, no. 1 (1988): 24. See also John Coulson,
Religion and Imagination: "In Aid of a Grammar of Assent" (Oxford:
Clarendon, 1981).

28. Newman, *Grammar of Assent*, 78, 291; *A Reason for the Hope*, 284-85, 289.

29. Newman, *A Reason for the Hope*, 282, 284-86.

would be a fruitful aspect of faith to explore directly. Newman was on to something that would prove to be extremely fruitful in the hands of William Lynch.

Newman's thinking was vastly different from the Scholastics. It was experientially based, accommodating both reason and feeling, and it was concerned with the faith of the simple as well as the learned. The personalist concerns that occupied Newman's attention would eventually be taken up by those who explored the Modernist turn to the subject.

III. The Modernist Challenge

The Modernist movement, dating roughly from 1890 to 1907, constituted the most important response to Scholastic integralism. Unfortunately, the term "Modernist" describes a rather disparate collection of scholars, some of whom ardently desired to remain faithful to the church, and others who departed quite decisively. Although the movement was present in Italy and to some extent in Germany, the most notorious Modernist activity took place in France and England.

The element that is common to virtually all interpretations of Modernism is that the movement represented an attempt to adapt the Church to the modern world. Modernists generally thought that Scholastics were too optimistic about the possibility of attaining a "pure" objectivity. Consequently, they focused on the turn to the subject. Such a profound shift threatened to alter the very notion of faith. Modernists thus proposed a paradigm shift in certain fundamental notions such as "truth" and, therefore, "faith." Truth as the correspondence of a mind to an object was challenged by a concept of truth as the adequacy of a concept in conveying the subjective experience of life itself. With such a concern, the absoluteness, immutability and objectivity of Scholasticism was challenged by the relativity, mutability and subjectivity of Modernism. Hence, the crisis has been viewed rightly as a confrontation between the newly developing historical consciousness and the old classical consciousness.[30]

Such a clash of worldviews reflected the age-old problem of the reconciliation of opposites. Daly sees the fundamental problem as the attempt to reconcile immanence and transcendence, the historical and the eternal, feeling and reason. Talar considers the clash in terms of nature and grace. Most interesting for our purposes is the observation of Paul Claudel that the Modernist crisis resulted from the Scholastic contempt for imagination and sensibility. He called it a tragedy of a "starved imagination" that could not keep together heaven and earth, feeling and reason, spirit and body, grace and nature, and idea and image.[31] On the other hand, William Lynch, in a passing reference, described Modernism in terms of the "psychologizing imagination," which reduced dogma to a set of symbols intended to produce mere religious affectivity without any concern for objective truth.[32]

A. Alfred Loisy

Alfred Loisy was no stranger to controversy. His services as Scripture professor at the newly formed Institut Catholique de Paris became mired in arguments relating to the disturbing implications of the historical-critical methods. Loisy had argued that the exegete's work must not be controlled by the foregone conclusions of dogma. History must retain a certain autonomy. Indeed, he claimed that the opening chapters of Genesis are not to be taken as literal history and that the Scriptures were bound by the same limitations that affected the writings of any other ancient author.[33]

---

30. Bernard Scott, introduction to *Gospel and the Church,* by Alfred Loisy (Philadelphia: Fortress, 1976), xxvii; Daly, *Transcendence and Immanence,* 227, C. J. T. Talar, *Metaphor and Modernist: The Polarization of Alfred Loisy and His Neo-Thomist Critics* (Lanham Md.: University Press of America, 1987), 28-29; Roger Haight, "The Unfolding of Modernism in France: Blondel, Laberthonnière, and Le Roy," *Theological Studies* 35, no. 4 (December, 1974) 632.

31. Daly, *Transcendence and Immanence,* 2, 31, 227; Talar, *Metaphor and Modernist,* 7-8, 24, 26, 33; Gerald A. McCool, "Twentieth-Century Scholasticism," in *Celebrating the Medieval Heritage,* ed. D. Tracy, *Journal of Religion* 58 (Supplement 1978): S204-S206; Paul Claudel, *Positions et propositions* in *Oeuvres Completes,* vol. 15 (France: Librairie Gallimard, 1959), 98-99.

32. William Lynch, *Christ and Apollo: The Dimensions of the Literary Imagination* (Notre Dame: University of Notre Dame Press, 1960), p. 9. Hereinafter cited as CA.

33. Bernard Scott, "Loisy and Modernism," in *The Gospel and the Church,* by Alfred

Ostensibly in response to Harnack's claim that the developments of Christianity were due to centuries of distortion, Loisy
proposed that Christianity and its doctrines legitimately grow with
history. He noted that the kernel of faith does not remain a seed.
It grows into a flowering plant that bears a relationship of continuity, not identity, with the past. The historian was to look for the
legitimate developments, the flower, not the seeds, as the seasons
passed. Therefore, the Gospel of the first century finds its legitimate
continuation in the Church which is quite different from the original
Christian community. Although intended as a defense of Catholicism, those arguments shocked many theologians because they
appeared to leave the Church without a transcendent reference. It
seemed to be completely a creature of history.

Insisting that he could speak only as an exegete and not as
a systematic theologian, Loisy presented his thought often in
ambiguous ways. For example, he was willing to allow that in a
certain sense miracles could prove the divine mission of Jesus,
yet he insists that every miracle is exaggerated. Some miracles
cannot be considered as historical at all. Furthermore, his findings
often seemed to leave no room for the transcendent. After
describing the Hellenization of Jewish Christianity, Loisy specu-
lated that Jesus became the Word made flesh only as a result of
the "spontaneous effort of the faith to define itself through the
necessary exigencies of propagandism."[34] In such wording, the
divine element of revelation seemed to be lacking. Indeed, the
very development of the Church appears in Loisy's writings to be
a result of the mere force of circumstances.

Loisy claimed that any ideas of God are merely anthropo-
morphisms. The intellect's approach to God is propelled by a
"religious instinct" that is innate in a person. A universal sense of
powerlessness brings people to submit themselves before God.[35]
Not only Catholicism but all religions result from divine revelation, and not merely from the subjective projections of the

Loisy, trans. C. Home, ed. B. Scott (Philadelphia: Fortress, 1976), xix.

34. Alfred Loisy, *Gospel and the Church*, trans. and ed. B. Scott (Philadelphia:
    Fortress, 1976), 40, 42, 50, 118-19, 192-93.

35. A. Firmin [Alfred Loisy], "La Definition de la religion," *Revue du clergé francais*
    18 (1899): 203f., 206-7.

believer.[36] God is at work within the human, but necessarily according to the human condition, which included intellectual and moral development.[37]

It was difficult for Scholastics to fathom how those theories could be consistent with supernatural faith. The Scholastics had argued that the truths of faith could be completely detached from the contingencies of history. Truth could not change. Loisy sensed that the historical was being slighted, but he did not clearly and persuasively explain the relationship of the divine to history. He was expelled from his teaching position at the Institut Catholique in 1893. Five of his books were eventually placed on the Index, and he was excommunicated in 1908.

B. Maurice Blondel

Beginning with his 1893 dissertation, Maurice Blondel also challenged the adequacy of the Scholastic thinking on faith, but not on the grounds of its handling of Scripture. Instead, he began to explore an alternative philosophical basis for religious thought. He shifted attention from the objective to the subjective concerns of the believer.

Blondel investigated the most intensely subjective aspect of a person's life: the quality of willing as it involves the entire person. There is a disproportion within the heart of every believer. On the one hand, there is the "willing will" (*"volonté voulante"*) by which all are continually drawn in an attempt to finally and decisively satisfy the deepest longings of the heart. On the other hand, there is the "willed will" (*"volonté voulue"*) by which we make individual choices in an attempt to satisfy the willing will. The problem is that the common experience of mankind indicates that the gap between those two aspects of the will remains, and, in fact, can even widen, in spite of the best efforts of the willed will to satisfy the heart. That dynamism, or vital immanence, either suggests the infinite in a person's life, or

36. A. Firmin [Alfred Loisy], "L'Idée de la revelation," *Revue du clergé francais* 21 (1899): 251.

37. Alfred Loisy, *Autour d'un petit livre* (Paris: Alphonse Picard et Fils, Editeurs, 1903), 195.

life is absurd. Philosophy, therefore, needs to be open to its existence if it adopts the position that human life makes sense.[38]

Even though faith, for Blondel, was found in the context of the disproportion of the will,[39] he was no subjectivist. Blondel insisted that revelation comes not from the self, but from the outside. To the extent that dogma expresses divine revelation, it serves as a vehicle to prompt the action of faith. Furthermore, dogma can renew people who otherwise might lose themselves "in a vague and floating aspiration after an infinite."[40] The truth of meaning must come from outside the person, and, as such, faith requires submission. The "Other" acts through whatever intermediary suits the divine purpose.

Faith comes into play when Blondel considered how it might be possible to bring into ourselves an idea or a life other than our own. How is union with God possible? Aiming at the very heart of Scholastic theory, Blondel shifted the focus of faith from intellection to action:

> For it is not from thought that faith passes over into the
> heart, it is from practice that it draws down a divine light
> for the spirit. God acts in this action and that is why the

---

38. Maurice Blondel, *Action (1893): Essay on a Critique of Life and a Science of Practice*, trans. Oliva Blanchette (Notre Dame: University of Notre Dame Press, 1984), 3, 365. Blondel was careful to distinguish his *method* of immanence from the *doctrine* of immanence. The method of immanence constituted a way of approaching the divine by noticing its affects in our subjective lives. The doctrine of immanence, which Blondel rejected, taught that the real was confined to this world, and intimations of the divine are only projections of human needs and desires. The *principle* of immanence, which Blondel seems to have accepted, held that before any idea or feeling can enter a person, it must adapt itself to that person's experience or way of perceiving. Cf. Daly, *Transcendence and Immanence*, 39, n. 39. The doctrine of immanence excluded the transcendent as objective reality. The method of immanence required the transcendent in order to make sense of human experience.

39. Contrary to Billot and Bainvel, Blondel insisted that the psychology of religious faith differs from the psychology of natural faith. The role of grace is discernible precisely in the restlessness of the heart, the disproportion of the will, the action that sets us on a search. One cannot confine faith simply to the intellect, to the will, or to grace (as if it could operate by itself). It is in the synthesis that the act of faith is completed. Maurice Blondel, "Retrieving the Tradition: What Is Faith?", trans. G. Connolly, Communio 2 (Summer 1987): 173, 191.

40. Blondel, *Action*, 376, 368.

thought that follows the act is richer by an infinity than that which precedes it.[41]

Truths that are mysterious, paradoxical and ironic become integrated into a person's life not through argument, but through action. These types of truths are "higher than reason."[42] Having done the truth, that person now knows it from the inside. Through the action that is the submission of faith, the divine is contained in the human, the transcendent in the immanent. As such, the divine could be seen as "more than universal" since "it is particular at each point and wholly within us." For Blondel, grace is present throughout the entire act of faith, and serves as the supernatural formal object or "light" by which a person comes to believe. It is the union of God and the believer, the very penetration of God into the source of our thought and action.[43]

Scholastics asserted that the act of faith was reasonable because it could be shown that God has spoken especially through reference to such "established facts" as miracles and prophecies.[44] But apologetics cannot simply rely on miracles and prophecies as if they will be equally convincing to all people. Apologetes must respect the inner experience of a person's life and the ways people naturally come to believe anything. Hence, contrary to the Scholastics, Blondel asserted that philosophy is not merely the dumb tool of theology. As Loisy asserted a certain autonomy for historical-critical research, so too Blondel claimed an autonomy for philosophy when it operates in its own sphere.[45]

---

41. Ibid., 367.
42. Ibid., 373, 376.
43. Blondel, "Retrieving the Tradition: What Is Faith?" 187-88, 191; Blondel, *Action*, 378.
44. Blondel, *Action*, 364-65; For Blondel, the value of miracles lay in their ability to provoke and to mortify believers into a submission of the self to the divine, and in their power to act as analogues of the supernatural. "L'Unité complexe du probléme de la foi: Méprise et élcairissements," *Revue du clergé francais* 53 (Feb. 7, 1908): 259, 276. Blondel affirmed the real nature of miracles and their probative value for those who saw them, but not apart from the action of grace. See "What Is Faith?" 179-80; *History and Dogma*, 277.
45. Philosophy is to "determine the content of thought and the postulants of action, without containing that life of which it analyzes the requirements...." Maurice Blondel, *The Letter on Apologetics*, in *The Letter on Apologetics and History and*

Blondel proposed that the synthesis of the natural and supernatural, of history and dogma, resides in a tradition that does not consist of additional truths that are passed on by word of mouth. Tradition is neither a "sacred stone" that is handed down from generation to generation nor is it the "sediment accumulated" through centuries of religious thought. Rather Tradition presents truth as lived, as acted, as known from the inside. Tradition preserves the continuity of both the doing of history and the knowing of dogma. In that way, the faith is not only transmitted, but it grows as a seed.[46] William Lynch will produce a similar notion of Tradition that reflects his concern to preserve the faith as a way of living that exhibits certain sensibilities that arise from practice, not merely from intellectual instruction. Indeed, he will propose that there is a unity of sensibility that characterizes the life of the faithful person.

Relying on Vatican I, Victor Dechamps, and John Henry Newman, Blondel offered a notion of faith that is a synthesis of knowing, willing and loving in relation to God. A believer knows the First Truth not as a simple object of study, but as a person who addresses us and expects a commitment through an adherence of the whole of one's being. The First Truth is loved as good, and that affects our knowledge of God as true. The God of philosophy, God as Truth, becomes the God of the Gospel as the

---

Dogma, trans. A. Dru and I. Trethowan (New York: Holt, Rinehart and Winston, 1964), 182, 196.

46. Blondel was clearly disturbed by the arguments presented by both Loisy and the Scholastics. Simplifying Loisy's position excessively, Blondel considered it as "historicism" that attempts to give a completely immanent, "objective" reading to historical narratives as if they contained only so many "brute" facts that could be read without a transcendent meaning. Opposed to historicism, Scholastics proposed a "dogmatism" or "extrinsicism" that considered the truths of faith as timeless, ahistorical, and unaffected by the culture in which they first appeared. Dogmatism is wrong, since the truths of the faith were meant to be lived from the inside. There is an inexplicable element of knowledge by connaturality that comes from action, not words. On the other hand, "historicism," is wrong in that it ignores the fact that dogmas come from a living Tradition whereby the significant element consists in people's ability to find God through the practice of that Tradition. There is a unity of life and thought in the faith that needs to be respected. Maurice Blondel, *History and Dogma* in *Letter on Apologetics and History and Dogma*, trans. A. Dru and I. Trethowan (New York: Holt, Rinehart and Winston, 1964), 277-78, 283, 287.

believer wholeheartedly begins to practice the faith in a real act of self-surrender. Then abstract theories can take on flesh and can become concretely realized. Then a certain "impression of reality" will inform the faith of the believer.[47] Lynch will consistently promote the importance of taking abstract doctrine and expressing it in real, concrete terms.

The certitude of faith "exceeds" that of science because it is a different type of certitude. In science, one consents to follow the evidence, no matter where it leads. The matter at hand is exterior, and consent can be required or forbidden based on the results of properly rigorous experiments regardless of the desires of the scientist. On the other hand, the interior fact is decisive in questions of faith and its certitude. In faith, assent is determined by the will. Faith's assent confers a type of certitude that allows a person to live wholeheartedly, and not hesitantly, as if only on the basis of a probability. Its certitude is not extrinsic, but intrinsic to the assent of the will.[48]

The complex unity of faith not only draws together intellect and will but also combines the natural and supernatural. Blondel continued to reject the compartmentalized apologetic of the Scholastics as if what were known through natural processes could be set aside when one makes a supernatural act of faith. The natural and supernatural origins of faith interpenetrate. Distinctions are necessary, but separations cause a "murderous vivisection" of faith. Blondel recalled Dechamps' admonition that the natural is already ordered to the supernatural, which attracts us and offers its divine light to us.[49]

---

47. Blondel, "What Is Faith?" 171, 173, 186.
48. F. Mallet [Maurice Blondel], "L'Unité complexe," 269, 270-71. Drawing on Dechamps, Blondel asserted that the interior fact of each person's life consists of the "consciousness of the Divine testimony within bidding us to believe." That interior fact may be considered as the person's practical good will, righteous living, docility to infused aspirations, or grace. The exterior fact alone cannot explain belief. Neither can the meeting of the interior and exterior facts. Faith consists essentially in the synthesis of the two that results in the mutual self-giving of the human and divine. Idem., "What Is Faith?" 183, 187, 190.
49. Blondel, "L'Unité complexe," 275; *Letter*, 147, 180.

Many of the crucial issues raised by Blondel were also raised by Lynch. Both proceed from the modern notion of truth. Both see that contraries need to be kept together in paradoxical ways, especially as they consider the implications of particular, concrete action. Whereas Blondel looked to action as the most telling aspect of a person's life, Lynch will look to its theatrical analogue: drama. While both respect the supernatural quality of faith, both grant an autonomous role to secular pursuits, such as philosophy and the arts. Both saw a vital dynamism at work within the human – Blondel in terms of the disproportion between an infinite dynamism and the daily decisions of the will, and, as we will see, Lynch in terms of the one and the many. Although Lynch does not appear to have relied explicitly on Blondel's work, it would seem that they were intellectual brothers.

Although Blondel spent many more productive years, his works during the Modernist period are generally considered to be his most profound. There was quite enough in Blondel's thought to catch the attention of Scholastics. Indeed, his friend, Lucien Laberthonnière, criticized Blondel's later apparent willingness to retreat from his philosophical program in the face of pressure from the Scholastics. It must be noted, however, that Blondel was never censured for his work, in fact, he was even commended by Pius XII for it. Nevertheless, Blondel's agenda and method were very suspicious to Scholastic theologians. When other theologians began to make use of Blondelian terminology, Scholastics became even more concerned.

C. Friederich von Hügel

Friederich von Hügel, a Scriptural exegete, entered the discussion supporting much of the technical work of Loisy but also adopting much of the Blondelian framework. Von Hügel seemed to be in touch with many of the forward-thinking scholars of his day, and thus influenced and encouraged other Modernists, most notably George Tyrrell.

For von Hügel the human and divine are neither separated nor identical. The relationship is "panentheistic." The absolute is experienced through the contingent. The point of faith for him is contained in "dim Experience," a point midway between reflex knowledge and ignorance. With some reflection, "dim Experience" reveals the presence of the Infinite. The analysis is similar to Blondel's method of immanence. There is a sense, not only of frustration, but also of "that which outleaps" our finite attempts. The finite self senses a "contrasting Other," which must be part of the experience of the contingent relative series of events. We feel the sting of contingency only because we have a sense for that which is not contingent. Faith in God, therefore, is not opposed to the definite. In fact, the infinite requires the finite to manifest itself.[50] Von Hügel reasons that nature and grace must not be radically separated, but different aspects of the same reality. As Dechamps maintained, ". . . human nature is not and never has been, although it might have been, in a condition of 'pure nature' . . . ."[51]

Ultimately, the divine reality is not fully comprehensible, and, therefore, cannot be conveyed in any one experience or conception. Von Hügel asserted that any language about the divine must deny as it affirms. It must speak in terms of analogy. Von Hügel also recognized that the experience of faith is so rich that no single faculty could contain it. All the faculties, including the imagination, need to interpenetrate to receive and express faith in God.[52]

Hence, when von Hügel discussed the elements and corresponding stages of religion as consisting of the sensed fact (which employs the imagination), the reasoned system (which employs the intellect), and the felt life or action (which employs the intuition), he again considered the interpenetration of faculties at work at each stage throughout a believer's life. Faith reflects that structure, but in an integrated way. To be sure, all the "parts" do not fit neatly together. There is a "tension" or a "friction" that attends to the believer's attempt to come to terms with the dynamic activity of the infinite in his or her life, but it is a fruitful tension.[53]

50. Friederich von Hügel, "Experience and Transcendence," *Dublin Review* 138 (April, 1906): 358-59, 360, 361-62, 363-64, 374; *Essays and Addresses on the Philosophy of Religion*, First Series (New York: E. P. Dutton, 1921), 115.

51. Quoted in Von Hügel, "Experience and Transcendence," 369.

52. Ibid., 375-76.

Throughout his thought, Lynch will demonstrate a deep conviction that would support von Hügel's theories on the relationship of the infinite and finite, on the necessity for analogical language, and on the integrated way in which the believer's faculties become interrelated in the act of faith. Much of that agenda was also carried forward by George Tyrrell, a priest deeply influenced by von Hügel.

D. George Tyrrell

In George Tyrrell's efforts to express the unity of the immanent and the transcendent, we find a theology that is replete with images. Lynch would consider many of the issues raised by Tyrrell to be of the utmost importance.

Tyrrell contended that God is offered to us in the concrete through action, not thought. Love is the action that is revelatory of God. Thus, Tyrrell at one point boldly states that God speaks to the heart, not to the head.[54] Although such overstatements, taken in isolation, made easy targets for Scholastic opponents, Tyrrell was stressing an aspect of faith that they had overlooked. Any image of God considered simply as image is an idol. The task of philosophy is to expose the inadequacy of the image while avoiding the replacement of the old concrete image with the abstract system that can become a new idol. Indeed, biblical images constitute the norm for faith, not the idols of faith. Theology must both critique and be faithful to those images just as the rules of English grammar must both critique and be faithful to English.[55]

But the critical function of theology can accomplish only so much. Relying on St. Thomas, Tyrrell explained that there is "no common or identical measure" between the attributes that describe God and those that describe creatures. The measure is one of analogy, or of proportion. God is "the hidden synthesis of irrecon-

---

53. Friederich von Hügel, *The Mystical Element of Religion as* Studied in Saint Catherine *of Genoa and Her Friends,* vol. 1 (New York: E. P. Dutton, 1927), 53-54.

54. George Tyrrell, *Lex Orandi* (New York: Longmans, Green, 1903), 48, 50; *External Religion: Its Use and Abuse* (London: Sands, 1903), 158.

55. George Tyrrell, *The Faith of Millions,* First Series (New York: Longmans, Green, 1901), 237, 239, 251-52.

cilables; we affirm that the synthesis exists, but of its nature we have no proper idea." A tree and the thought of a tree do not share any real content, yet there is an analogous resemblance by which each can be used to refer to the other. Theological language is like that except for the fact that God is not known as an object but as the subject, who is both immanent and transcendent.[56]

One type of analogous truth concerns fictions. They can promote the spiritual life because of their value as proper analogues between the natural and the supernatural. Their truth is found by their fruitfulness.[57] For example, if we were to ask whether the Synoptic dating of the Last Supper is true as opposed to the Johannine dating, Tyrrell might well respond that they are both true. That is, there is a profound truth in considering the Last Supper as a Passover meal, but there is also a profound truth in timing it so that the crucifixion of Jesus coincides with the slaying of the Passover lambs. The chronology is not the point; it is merely an "illusion" or a "fiction," but not a pure fiction because there is a deeper analogical truth at stake.

Tyrrell was aware that simple intuition could not be trusted. One must rely on discursive reason as well. Even the intuition of a saint is not enough. For example, the Curé of Ars possessed wonderful purity of heart, giving him worthy intuitions. Yet his natural intelligence was not acute, and, Tyrrell observes, it led him to many theological errors. To such a saint, one must say, "Give me your opinion, but don't give me your reasons."[58] Tyrrell noted that critical reason must be brought to bear on the images of faith to expose our naive initial understanding of a text. But one cannot remain simply at the critical level:

> [a] deeper and more comprehensive theology seems in most cases to bring us back to our original point of departure, albeit on a higher plane; to restore to us the stimulus of our childlike conceptions, not only fully, but superabundantly; and to convince us almost experimen-

---

56. Tyrrell, *Lex Orandi*, 81-82.
57. Ibid., 57-58.
58. George Tyrrell, *Nova et Vetera: Informal Meditations* (New York: Longmans, Green, 1900), 169, 355.

tally, that God's way of putting the truth was, after all, the better and wiser.[59]

Years later, Paul Ricoeur would propose the very same principle by advising us that the images of faith, once naively accepted at face value, need to undergo a rational analysis that will expose the weaknesses of the naive interpretation. He too will encourage readers to return to the faith images with a postcritical naiveté, that is, a renewed openness to be carried away by the story but with a more confident sense for its true direction.[60] Lynch will propose the same dynamic in terms of images that require us to undergo a descent into hell before we rise to new insight.

Unfortunately, Tyrrell's writing was vivid enough and, at times, ambiguous enough, and certainly anti-Scholastic enough to attract unsympathetic interpreters. Tyrrell's works were placed on the Index, and in 1907 he was excommunicated.

IV. The Scholastic Reaction to Modernism

The Scholastic reaction was swift and zealous. The Modernist turn to the subject threatened the metaphysical and epistemological system that had been constructed so carefully in response to pastoral, doctrinal, and political concerns. Scholastics saw their integralist approach to truth as unchanging, complete, and divinely guaranteed, a groundwork that would provide the basis for a clear, distinct and objective apologetic through which the faith could be defended. That groundwork was soon spelled out by the Vatican.

A. *Pascendi* and *Lamentabili*

On July 3, 1907, the Holy Office published *Lamentabili Sane*, a syllabus condemning specified errors of Modernism. Throughout the document, there is a consistent refusal to recognize that truth

---

59. Tyrrell, *Faith of Millions*, 247.
60. Paul Ricoeur, *Interpretation Theory: Discourse and the Surplus of Meaning* (Fort Worth: Texas Christian University Press, 1976), 74. Hereinafter cited as "*IT*."

is historical. For example, the findings of the historical-critical methods are explicitly rejected (DS 3403, 3412). God is considered to be the author of Scripture in a simple, straightforward sense (DS 3409). The truths taught by Christ are applicable to all people at all times in all places without need of adaptation (DS 3459). In spite of what Loisy claimed, the discourses of Jesus, and his miracles, are reported accurately (DS 3416-3417). Furthermore, Scripture contains no fiction intended merely for the spiritual benefit of its readers (DS 3414). Truth has indeed fallen from heaven, so there is no distinction between the "Christ of faith" and the "Christ of history" (DS 3422, 3429).

Unfortunately, *Lamentabili* was only the first volley, signaling that the heavy artillery was yet to be fired. On September 8, 1907, Pius X issued the encyclical *Pascendi Dominici Gregis,* which presented a Scholastic version of Modernism and the steps that needed to be taken to correct the errors. As the compendium of all errors, Modernism was accused of both rationalism and fideism. It was rationalist insofar as it seemed to reject whatever appeared miraculous and timeless, and it was fideist since the decision to believe seemed to be based on interior feelings.

Pius X expressed deep pastoral concern over the inability to control the results of the historical-critical methods at the level of the common parishioner. Once a single biblical fact is admitted to be historically false, anyone could select only the passages that were amenable to that individual and ignore the rest (ASS 629). Truth is one, and to divide that unity is pernicious and false (ASS 629).

Pascendi attacked the Modernist notion of truth as lived experience. Such a notion was thought to lead to the complete separation of faith and science. Consequently, Modernists were considered to be agnostics (ASS 596). Faith was seen as merely the projected response to a subjective interior need (ASS 597, 600, 623). The principle of vital immanence, through which revelation is found by virtue of the needs present within an individual's life, was considered as a sort of epistemology based on the fickleness of the heart (ASS 597-598). The intellect's role was consigned to merely picturing or symbolizing that interior sense (ASS 601). Dogmas are not made to fit the truth but are adapted to the heart (ASS 599-600, 602).

For the Modernist, God is found strictly in this world. *Pascendi* applied a syllogism to the Modernist: "It is handed on by the philosopher that *the principle of faith is immanent*; from the believer it is added that *this principle is God*; and he [the theologian] draws the conclusion: therefore *God is immanent in man.*"[61] Such is the doctrine of immanence. However, *Pascendi* notes that some Modernists appear to use "immanent" in the approved Augustinian sense in which God is considered to be more intimately present to the believer than the person is even to himself or herself ("quod Deus agens intime adsit in homine, magis quam ipse sibi homo") (ASS 610). Apparently referring to Blondel, *Pascendi* stated that there are Catholics who reject the doctrine of immanence, while employing the method of immanence. They employ that imprudent apologetic that concentrates on the compelling need that human nature has for the supernatural order. While complaining that such apologetical methods ought not to be desired in Catholic circles, *Pascendi* tagged apologetes who employ that method as "moderate" Modernists (ASS 630).

Pascendi concluded with a disciplinary admonition requiring the use of Scholastic philosophy as the basis for all Catholic theology. Bishops were directed to examine all Catholic publications carefully and to be most judicious in issuing the *Imprimatur*, lest the poison of Modernism spread any further. Diocesan Councils of Vigilance were also to be convened to keep close watch for the safety of the flock to see that its food remain pure, an important concern for an encyclical entitled *Pascendi Domini Gregis* ("Of the Feeding of the Lord's Flock") (ASS 593).

Modernists generally denied that the condemned propositions adequately described their individual theological positions. Over some misgivings by Laberthonnière that too much was being conceded, Blondel clarified his stance on the method of immanence. George Tyrrell gave his response in the oft-quoted quip that, although *Pascendi* "tries to show the Modernist that he is no Catholic, it mostly succeeds only in showing him that he is no

---

61. "Traditur a philosopho *principium fidei esse immanens*; a credente additur *hoc principium Deum esse*: concludit ipse *Deus* ergo *est immanens in homine*" ASS 609.

scholastic." Loisy claimed the rendition of Modernism offered by *Pascendi* was a "fictional system." Von Hügel maintained the interesting position of calling himself a Modernist for the first time in 1908, but also expressing an ardent devotion to the Church.[62]

By September 1, 1910, three years after the appearance of *Pascendi*, the Oath Against Modernism (DS 3537-3550) was published and required of all clerics and other office-holders in the Church. It rejected agnosticism, the evolution of dogmas, rationalism, fideism, text criticism, and the ability of history to disprove the faith as understood in the time of Christ. It mandated the acceptance of the external proofs of revelation, Christ's founding of the Church with Peter as its head, and the absolute truth that has always existed in the episcopal succession from the Apostles. The document was so succinct and carried such practical weight that it became a handy reference for dogmatic purity.

B. Thomas Aquinas

Although Thomas' writings are commonly available today, it was only toward the turn of the 20th century that scholars began to have access to Thomas's system so it could be applied to modern concerns. A brief sketch of Thomas's thought on faith will enable us to consider how Scholasticism was prompted to change in light of the retrieval of Thomism.

Faith in the time of Thomas was threatened by many factors, including a new awareness of the power of Eastern religions, state interference in dogmatic concerns, a reassessment of faith in light of a renewed interest in Scripture, and political instability. Aristotle's thought had recently been introduced by way of contacts with the Arab world, and through it, much of the symbolic thinking of the Middle Ages was criticized. The consideration of nature as valuable in itself, and not merely as a symbol of a divine attribute, threatened to de-divinize the universe.

Thomas responded by fashioning an accommodation between the best offered by the Tradition and the best offered by Aristotle. Thomas thought it possible to speak of the supernatural

---

62. Daly, *Transcendence and Immanence*, 204-7.

without excluding the natural. That concern appeared to be operative in his discussion on faith. He defined the interior act of faith as ". . . an act of the intellect assenting to divine truth at the command of the will moved by the grace of God" ($ST\,2^a2^{ae}$, q. 2, art. 9, resp.). Faith is neither vision nor deductive knowledge, since in such cases a person knows and does not believe. Faith is also different from mere opinion, since opinion is devoid of firm assent and is plagued by fears that the other side of the issue may be correct ($ST\,2^a2^{ae}$, q. 2, art. 1, resp.). While faith does not doubt, there is a mental unrest that is provoked by the dissatisfaction of the mind that desires to see what it believes. It constitutes a type of probing of what has become the object of one's absolute love ($ST\,2^a2^{ae}$, q. 2, art. 1, ad. 1-3).

The clarity of faith is attained by its formal object, or the principle by which faith is grasped, namely, the First Truth. We believe God. Its material object, the content of faith, is also the First Truth. We believe in God. It is only by virtue of God's grace, by hearing God's revelation, and by feeling an inward attraction, that a person comes to faith ($ST\,2^a2^{ae}$, q. 2, art. 2, resp.). Considered from the viewpoint of the formal and material object, faith is more certain than science. Considered from the viewpoint of the subject, faith is less certain because matters of faith are above the human intellect ($ST\,2^a2^{ae}$, q. 4, art. 8, resp.).

While the evidences of miracles and prophecies are important signs that can lead a person to faith, they remain only external inducements, and not self-sufficient proofs. After all, people can see the same miracle; some believe while others do not. Hence, the inward cause is decisive. Of course, a dispositive cause needs to clear away any unreasonable prejudices against faith. Once that is accomplished, that inward cause by which a person begins a new life is God moving the person by grace ($ST\,2^a2^{ae}$, q. 6, art. 1).

Signs of credibility, of course, can help. Indeed, some outward sign is necessary. A person must have some grounds for believing. It is not simply an arbitrary act. However, those rational motives do not amount to a demonstration of faith because the object in that case would be seen. Evidences merely remove obstacles to faith ($ST\,2^a2^{ae}$, q. 2, art. 10, ad. 2-3). In answer to an objection that believing is seeing, Thomas replied that when the things of faith are considered particularly, they cannot be seen and believed at the same time. It would amount to a contradiction in terms. However, considered generally, the believer "sees" in the sense that there is a content that appears credible to him. No one believes without seeing that what is being proposed ought to be believed. There is no separate judgment of credibility that must be made prior to the act of faith. Credibility is merely a "general aspect" of the matters of belief (*ST* 2^a2^{ae}, q. 1, art. 4, ad. 2).[63]

Thomas also proposed that the believer benefits from a certain "*interiori instinctu Dei,*" or a spontaneous inclination imposed by a higher agency whereby a being tends to act in a way that achieves what is good for it, and avoids what is evil (*ST* 2^a2^{ae}, q. 2, art. 9, ad. 3; q. 6, art. 1). As sheep flee from wolves and seek out green pastures, so too people are inclined naturally to the vision of God. Furthermore, once the grace of faith is accepted, the believer sees by the light of faith (*ST* 2^a2^{ae}, q. 2, art. 3, resp.). Things then are seen as they are related to God. The light of faith is not an additional thing to be seen, but a new light by which to see. By connaturality one gains a feel for the faith and can simply recognize what the faith requires.

While it must be admitted that Thomas does take an intellectualist approach to faith, his thought is considerably more integrated into all the spiritual powers than that of the Scholastics.

C. Subsequent Catholic Theology

One of the practical effects of *Pascendi* was that further development in Catholic theology would take place only in a Thomistic context. Although Gardeil had experimented with the intuitive element in faith, he backed away from any attempt to integrate it into Catholic theology.

In 1908, Pierre Rousselot discovered the importance of the intuitive element in Thomas' philosophy thereby allowing a new breakthrough. Intellectual intuition is a form of sympathetic union with the nonself. Perfect intuition is identical with love. Hence,

---

63. See Guy de Broglie, "La vraie notion thomiste des 'praeambula fidei'," *Gregorianum* 34 (1953): 341-89; also in *Theology Digest* 7 (1959): 47-52.

there is a connaturality at play between the knower and the known in the intuitive element. Lynch will embrace precisely the same principle. For him, real knowledge is no different from love.[64]

It follows that the will is not so extrinsic to the intellect as had been supposed. The heart can charm the reason so that it transforms rational judgments for the better. For example, new knowledge comes with freely chosen occupations. A soldier will adopt a special point of view and will know his pair of boots differently from the way a shoemaker knows them. Each has different but valid knowledge. Rousselot concluded that the freedom of love and the certitude of knowledge interpenetrate.[65]

These discoveries enabled Rousselot as a Thomist to propose that faith results from a "reciprocal causality." Faith needs exterior facts and signs, but those facts will not speak of the truth of faith without the grace of the *lumen fidei*, the supernatural formal object of faith. The *lumen fidei* senses the whole so that individual facts can be seen in a new light. In a manner reminiscent of the way Newman approached this topic, Rousselot claimed that the situation might be likened to two detectives who view the same facts. The stray blade of grass can be a telling clue for one detective, but it may well leave the other stupefied. Both clues and story come simultaneously in one act of insight. Facts become clues as they begin to tell a story. There is a reciprocal causality at work.[66]

Faith is contained in that moment of insight when the believer catches on to a new synthesis, a new way that reality can fit together. Once it is seen, it appears not only rational but certain. That new synthesis can, with the help of grace, be motivated in any number of ways. Just as the stray blade of grass can bring everything together for the intellectually acute detective, so too even a blade of grass can send into ecstasy those in whom the light of faith gleams brightly. That is to say, faith varies according to the *lumen fidei*.[67]

---

64. P. Rousselot, *The Intellectualism of St. Thomas*, trans. James O'Mahoney, (New York: Sheed and Ward, 1935), 220. Idem., "Les Yeux de la foi," *Recherches de science religieuse* 1 (1910): 450-51, 456-57, 460, 464. William F. Lynch, "The Meaning of Mud," *Spirit: A Magazine of Poetry* 6, no. 6 (January, 1940): 178.

65. Pierre Rousselot, "Les Yeux de la foi," 450 n.1; 452-53, 457.

66. Ibid., 445 n.1; 250-52, 253-55.

Certainly Rousselot's concept of faith was criticized, but it is significant that it was developed from within a Thomistic context. Even though Rousselot's thoughts on faith were published the same year as the Oath Against Modernism, he was still able to highlight the subjective and intuitive dimensions of Thomistic epistemology at a time when those dimensions were most severely under attack. He and Joseph Maréchal developed the intuitive element of Thomistic epistemology and its positive interplay with the free will. Legitimate Kantian insights about the subjective nature of knowledge eventually could become integrated with the Thomistic sense for the intellect's ability to grasp the real. Those insights were later taken up by Karl Rahner and Bernard Lonergan in the development of what would become transcendental Thomism. William Lynch's theology of the imagination falls in line with this development, since his concern will focus on the images that become part of the cognitive and the affective life of the person. Reality is encountered in the reception and the fashioning of those images in one's culture.

With the developments initiated by Rousselot and Maréchal, the Thomistic world began to open its windows. Jacques Maritain and Etienne Gilson contributed much to the historical understanding of the thought of Thomas. Although Gilson remained skeptical of the subjective, Maritain returned to his earlier interest in the role of the intuition, and developed a Thomistic aesthetics. By 1935, theologians began to react against the "*Konklusiontheologie*" of the Scholastics. Dom Anselm Stolz, O.S.B., for example, suggested a theology based not on abstract systemization but on a fresh study of Scripture and Tradition. Theology, as a study of supernatural faith, should be considered a charism, a gift that edifies the faith of real believers rather than merely building more complex defenses and proofs for the scholars. Other theologians such as Joseph Jungmann and Hugo Rahner proposed that such a task be accomplished especially in view of the pastoral needs of the people to hear the effectively preached word. Hence, they developed a kerygmatic theology. Although not in dialogue with any particular theological school, William Lynch began at this time to publish

---

67. Ibid., 457-58, 460-61, 259.

articles concerning the ancient Greek classics, and the value of arts as capable of inspiring holiness, not only among the learned but also among the uneducated.

By the end of the Second World War, certain French theologians were calling for a *Nouvelle Theologie.* Jean Daniélou called for the Church to become "incarnate" in each culture. Life and theology must be joined by treating God as subject and not object, by treating the secular arts and sciences as having valuable input, and by adopting a concrete attitude to humanity. Henri de Lubac's *Surnaturel* recalled themes familiar to those who followed the Modernists and the developments of Rousselot's and Maréchal's thought. In that book, de Lubac reaffirmed that there is no separation between the natural and supernatural and that there is no "pure" nature in concrete human existence.

Such theologies were criticized by M. Labourdette as relativist and subjectivist. Particularly odious to Labourdette was de Lubac's penchant for incorporating modern literary, artistic, or aesthetic terms in which theology could be critiqued. M. J. Garrigou-Lagrange objected to the shift in the notion of truth from the adequation of a mind to a thing to the conformity of ideas to life. Eventually the debate became so heated that Rome intervened through the issuance of the encyclical *Humani Generis.*

In that encyclical, Pius XII reaffirmed the excellence of the Scholastic approach. He complained about the new theology's attempt to relate transcendent reality "by disparate teachings . . . although they are in a certain way mutually opposed to each other" ("quam disparatis doctrinis . . . quamvis sibi invicem quodammodo opponantur") (AAS 573). Rather than deal in immutable essences, the new theology claimed that "it is necessary to look to the 'existence' of things and to life, which is ever in flux" ("ad 'existentiam' singulorum spectet necesse est et ad vitam semper fluentem") (AAS 573).

It is clear that the imagination was considered to be among the many causes of that new confusion in theology. The intellect, claimed Pius XII, is hampered by the senses, the imagination, and the evil passions that arose from original sin (AAS 562). The imagination was considered as the opponent of truth.[68] Narratives in Scripture "must least of all be equated with myths or other such things which proceed more from an extravagant imagination than from the striving for truth and simplicity. . . ."[69] The purposes of theology and the Church are much better served by the perennial "traditional philosophy . . . with its clear description and solution of questions, its accurate definition of concepts, its clear-cut distinctions . . . admirably accommodated to the medieval mentality."[70]

Reaction to *Humani Generis* came quickly and obediently. The old Scholastic theology had won the day. Nevertheless, by 1954, Lynch was already proposing that theology be considered as an exercise of the "analogical imagination."[71] Within the decade, Pope John XXIII would open the windows to the fresh air of modern thought, so that such new directions in theology might be considered openly.

V. The Issues of Faith

Some time after Ichabod Crane's adventure, the story was being retold among the burghers of "Manhattoes." All were of good cheer except one individual who "never laughed but upon good grounds." This man of ill humor could not decide on the veracity of the tale even after hearing a syllogism containing a rather dubious moral. It seems that this individual more or less relived the tale in his head and struggled with the grounds of belief as

---

68. For a survey on thought on the imagination, especially as it was used by certain Protestant thinkers in the nineteenth century, see appendix 2.

69. "[E]a cum mythologiis aliisve id genus minime aequnda sunt, quae magis ex effusa imaginatione procedunt quam ex illo veritatis ac simplicitatis studio" (AAS 577.)

70. "Quare philosophiam nostris traditam scholis, cum sua lucida quaestionum, descriptione ac solutione, cum accurata sua notionum determinatione clarisque distinctionibus, . . . mentibus hominum medii aevi egregi accomodatum. . . ." (AAS 573). It is interesting that Pius XII had already issued *Divino Afflante Spiritu* (1943, DS 3825) thereby approving of the responsible use of historical critical methods in biblical research (DS 3826-3830). Such a profound shift in the treatment of scriptural images would certainly imply a like shift in theology, yet that shift appeared to be more difficult to acknowledge. It did not come until the issuance of *Mysterium Ecclesiae* under Paul VI in 1973.

71. William F. Lynch, "Theology and the Imagination," *Thought* 29, no. 112 (spring, 1954): 74ff.

one would struggle with deciding what makes a joke funny, if indeed it is.[72] Sometimes acts that are simple and spontaneous become complex and studied when justification is sought.

Throughout the period reviewed, theologians have struggled to retain the simplicity and sponteneity of faith, while at the same time proving it to be a rational act. The Scholastics, in their attempt to respond to rationalists, to preserve the faith of common believers, and to defend the Church from state interference, proposed a theology that sought refuge in the safety of a syllogism. In their effort to protect the objectivity of faith, their theology seemed to present, not the headless horseman of the fideists and traditionalists, but a horseman who carried his head in his hands: a head that was a ready weapon against the attacks of any disbelieving heart. The head of the Scholastics appeared to be a purely defensive organ that not geared at all to inspiring faith. Perhaps Blondel's claim that a "murderous vivisection" had occurred is an apt image for Scholasticism.

Various Modernists, while at times too critical of the need to justify faith rationally and at times too incautious philosophically, were eager to describe and justify faith as experienced subjectively at the moment of catching on to the new synthesis. For them faith constitutes either a new vision of the modern world or no vision at all. Such thought brought an analogous certitude, but not one conducive to extrinsic proofs.

The issues concerning faith seem to center around the reconciliation of opposites. Faith is an intensely subjective act but is moored to the objective realm as well. Faith brings people in touch with the transcendent, but never outside of the immanent. Faith traffics in the sacred, but does not bypass the secular. Faith conveys glad tidings for humankind in general, but does not abandon the concrete individual to do so. This list of contraries could be extended in terms of the natural and supernatural, the one and the many, certitude and pensiveness, the self and the cosmos, the will and the reason, the finite and the infinite, and many others.

The problem for theologians has not been *whether* to keep these opposites together. The problem is *how* to keep them

---

72. Irving, "The Legend of Sleepy Hollow," 359.

together. Some ways appear artificial because they result in the total suppression of one or the other terms of the duality. Other ways offer more promise because they combine opposites in ways that allow each term to make a unique contribution to enhance the whole. By his focus on imagination, William Lynch has offered insights that attempt a fruitful, convincing whole to emerge from the contraries that beset every human life. He has attempted to allow the simplicity and spontenaity of the joyful laugh of faith to remain while justifying its basis in reason.

CHAPTER TWO

Lynch's Theology of Interpenetration: The Analogical Imagination

IN HERMAN MELVILLE'S CLASSIC, *MOBY DICK*, WHEN THE WHALING ship *Pequod* neared the equator, Ahab took hold of his quadrant to assist him in finding his way. As he aligned the noon day sun in its sights, Ahab realized his frustration at his own finitude. The "high and mighty Pilot" in the heavens knew the location of the elusive White Whale but would not disclose it. In a rage, Ahab exclaimed,

> Science! Curse thee thou vain toy; and cursed be all things that cast man's eyes aloft to that heaven whose live vividness but scorches him . . . Level by nature to this earth's horizon are the glances of man's eyes . . . Curse thee thou quadrant!

Vowing to rely solely on the dead-level reckoning of the compass, Ahab dashed his quadrant to the deck: "Aye . . . thus I split and destroy thee!" Turning his attention from the Pilot of the heavens, "his live and dead feet" trampled the tool which had enabled this divided man to integrate the vertical with the horizontal, the source of life with the source of death, in his voyage on this earth.[1]

---

1. Herman Melville, *Moby-Dick; or The Whale* (New York: Penguin Books, 1972), chapter 118, pp. 609-610.

Is there such an instrument for the science of theology? Is there a method to keep both horizontal and vertical in view? Before turning to William Lynch's thoughts on faith, it will serve us well to inspect the capabilities of the instruments he has chosen to guide his ship through those hazardous waters. A worthy method will pay attention to both vertical and horizontal dimensions. It will value both quadrant and compass in reaching its assessment of the presence of the divine. As we will see, Lynch's method presents not a set of rules to follow, but, rather like compass and quadrant, it provides a continuing orientation to be maintained throughout a theological inquiry. Indeed, he has described its main component, analogy, not only as a tool but also as a habit or a practice.[2]

Since any method assumes a certain vision of reality in light of which the methodological tools make sense, first Lynch's fundamental assumptions regarding the structure of reality and the nature of knowing will be reviewed. Then the instruments he recommends for use will be laid out for our inspection.

I. Foundational Aspects of Lynch's Method

A. A Metaphysics of Interpenetration

The starting point in Lynch's method is the finite. He is convinced that the human avenue leading to the very depths of reality runs through concrete, finite reality. Once the finite has penetrated to the core, insights will result regarding not only the finite, but the infinite as well. All knowledge of God is mediated through finite objects, yet God is not known simply as an object. The divine is known only indirectly. Knowledge of the transcendent dimension is gained through our experience of the concrete world. Lynch is determined to show that the transcendent is an aspect of the immanent. One never simply uses the finite as a launching pad to skyrocket to some other sphere. There is no ego that "transcends itself" to go someplace else.[3] This world is the only one we have.

---

2. William F. Lynch, *The Integrating Mind: An Exploration into Western Thought* (New York: Sheed and Ward, 1962), 113, 116-7, 132. Hereinafter cited as "*IM*."

3. William F. Lynch, "The Problem of Freedom," *Cross Currents* 10 (spring 1960): 111.

But few recognize the infinite depth of this world. Any true voyage into this world already constitutes a voyage into what many would call the "next" world.[4]

How can this be? Lynch drew on St. Ignatius, Plato, and a study of Greek drama to explain his position. Lynch was confident that the finite should not be abandoned. For centuries retreatants have been advised by St. Ignatius' *Spiritual Exercises* to heighten their awareness of the divine through concentration on specific concrete facts. He was not interested in the construction of an "other" world. His way of spirituality was founded on a "theology of the penetration of this finite [world] into God."[5] Ignatius' spirituality assumed that God is not external to the human. He refused to be caught in the position of having to choose between God and the human as if a person could choose the one without choosing the other.[6]

Ignatius also recognized that finite reality comes to us only through time. Consequently, he divided the *Spiritual Exercises* into four "weeks." Temporality is part of the structure of reality as we know it. Hence, there is to be no cheating, no collapsing of reality as if we already knew the future. Exercitants are led "proportionately" through the life of Christ, that is, according to events as they happened in a definite sequence. The time structure of the *Exercises* implies a theology of action, since there is no time without action. Ignatius relied on concrete events, on the specific action that constituted the love of Jesus, to bring us into union with God. It is not just any treatment of the finite that brings us into touch with God. It is its treatment through the life of Christ that discloses the true depths of the finite.[7]

---

4. William F. Lynch, *Christ and Apollo: The Dimensions of the Literary Imagination* (Notre Dame: University of Notre Dame Press, 1960), xi, 7, 141. Hereinafter cited as "*CA*."

5. William F. Lynch, "Saint Ignatius and the 'New Theological Age'," *Thought* 31, no. 121 (Summer 1956): 197-98.

6. Ibid., 202, 204.

7. Ibid., 208-10; *CA* 54-59. Lynch described several modern efforts to escape the finite through an escape of time. See *CA* 31-53. Lynch's concept of time suggests that human temporality is a "movement into and within the infinite," a movement thoroughly imbedded in the processes of "living through experience," and a movement in which each point of illumination comes

Furthermore, Ignatius expected each moment of time to be treated in the fullness of its concrete actuality. All the contours and lines of the definite are to be considered. This so-called "composition of place" required the exercitants to "see the spot" where the event took place. They should compose it, and give it the qualities of the finite. Ignatius also counselled those in meditation to apply as many of the five senses as they could. These methods of becoming steeped in reality through becoming steeped in the finite were remarkably productive in the spiritual life. The Church even named Ignatius as "patron of retreats" in recognition of his success in this regard.[8]

Through his Ignatian spirituality, Lynch sensed that the deepest dimension of the finite is its ability to communicate the infinite. Ignatius gave him the experience, the insight, and the confidence that such is the case. Plato gave him the logical reasoning process by which it might be rendered philosophically intelligible. The problem posed itself as one of the oldest in all of philosophy: the unification of contraries. By "contrary," Lynch means that any finite entity is composed of certain "opposites" that contribute to the making of the thing. Those opposites are always found together in the thing. They are never separated, or found alone.[9] A simple example would be the contraries "left" and "right" which are opposing features of any physical entity. There is no left without a right, and vice versa. Contradictories, on the other hand, must be separated. They must be found in a separated state because the one contradictory tends to cancel the other. While contradictories may be found juxtaposed in a conflicted posture to each other, they are never together in the sense that contraries are. For example, while the contraries "good" and "bad" may be found together in the suffering of a good man (or in other ways that his goodness is naturally limited), "good" and "evil" would be contradictories because the one tends to banish the other.[10] Contraries are too often mistaken as contradictories.

---

sequentially, even consequentially, that is, each one is "necessary to and causative of the next" (*CA* 39). For a discussion of Lynch's concept of time, see Chapter Three, Section IV, "Faith and Time."

8. Lynch, "Saint Ignatius," 213-14.

9. Lynch, "Theology and Imagination," *Thought* 29, no. 112 (Spring 1954): 82ff.

Lynch could see that contraries included such pairs of opposites as the one and the many, the finite and the infinite, the immanent and the transcendent, the sacred and the secular, the same and the different, fear and trust, and many other relationships. The problem is that too many people consider those kinds of relationships as contradictory, and consider each term as separated from the other. When they attempt to put the terms back together, their efforts usually fail. Lynch's insight is that a person does not have to worry about putting together contraries that were never separated in the first place.[11]

How is it that we can experience in one and the same thing both the one and the many, both the finite and infinite, both fear and trust, or any other set of contraries?

For these purposes, Lynch turned to Plato's *Parmenides*, a conundrum-filled instrument that has been crashed against the decks of philosophy by more than one student who has attempted to align the sights of its widely divergent claims. Enticed by the challenge of making sense of what is considered as Plato's most difficult dialogue, Lynch produced a commentary that has been hailed as one of the most significant contributions on the subject this century.[12]

Lynch's excursus into Platonic metaphysics allowed him to take what was posited there with respect to the relationship between the one and the many and to apply it in religious terms to the finite and infinite. Within the very structure of the finite there exists, as its contrary, the infinite. The two are not confused, changed, divided or separated.[13] Just as the one cannot exist

---

10. *IM* 55, 102-5; William F. Lynch, *Images of Hope: Imagination as Healer of the Hopeless* (Notre Dame: University of Notre Dame Press, 1965), 229ff. Hereinafter cited as "*IH.*"

11. *IM* 176, *CA* 133.

12. Leonard Eslick, review of *An Approach to the Metaphysics of Plato Through the Parmenides*, by William F. Lynch, *Thought* 37, no. 144 (Spring 1962): 144. It should also be noted that Eslick disagreed with Lynch's development of a doctrine of participation in Plato's thought. See Appendix II for a detailed discussion of Lynch's treatment of *The Paremenides*.

13. Christology was one of Lynch's chief theological interests, *CA* xii-xiii. The parallel with the Chalcedonean formula would suggest that Christology could benefit from Lynch's analysis of contraries.

without the many, so too the finite cannot exist without the infinite. They are interpenetrating realities.

For example, if a visitor were to ask to see one's parish, the parishioner might bring that person to a liturgy, show the school, watch various committees in action, read the mission statement, drive around the neighborhood, meet the people and pastor, and so on. At the end of the day, one might imagine the visitor saying, "Thank you for showing me the liturgy, the people, the buildings, and the neighborhood, but now show me the parish." The visitor would have missed the point. There is not another thing to show. The "unity" called "parish" is found in its "many" articulations. Such is the relationship between the one and the many.

When God is considered in relation to creation, then God is the "One" in whom we as contingent "others" participate. The many exist only by virtue of the "one." In Plato's reflections on the one and the many, he correctly observed that the principle of unity gives meaning to the many. Even though there is no intervening principle that joins the one to the many, it is the principle of unity that organizes its members into a meaningful whole. In the example cited above, there is no parishioner without the greater unity called "the parish" which assembles in response to the call of Christ. The visitor might indeed miss the parish if its overriding principle of unity is not perceived. The one and the many are not co-absolute. A musical analogy might further clarify the relationship. The tune "Camptown Races" presents itself by virtue of the overall schema developed by Stephen Foster. Any individual note is incapable of ordering the notes around it. Each individual note lacks the perspective of the whole. Yet the music consists only of the many notes that make it up. The many are beholden to the one for their very existence. The parts share in the whole and gain their identity from the whole. The one organizes the many and gives them their very being. That is to say that the many contribute nothing to the "oneness" of the one. Only the one is one. It is not by virtue of the many that the one exists, but it is by virtue of the principle of unity that the many exist in a coherent, intelligible, ordered way. A sheer many is so indefinite that it is unintelligible.

Keeping Lynch's Platonic terminology in mind, it is more accurate to say that we are the "other" of God than to say that God is the "Other," a position we might easily adopt in light of Rudolf Otto's classic study on the holy as the "Wholly Other."[14] We are God's "other," God is not our "other." When God becomes an "other," a human being is the result. God is still a "unity and infinity" in the absolute sense, but God is also a "One" that can produce an "other" that relates as creation to God. Hence, people quite naturally address God as "One" who is a personal being to whom they might speak as if addressing another person.

Several corollaries follow. If we are the "other" of God, we may say that we are removed from God, but God is not removed from us. We are the estranged "ones," the estranged "many." Insofar as we are "many," we are a mixture of being and relative nonbeing. "Absolute Being" is God. In the absolute sense, Being has no contrary or contradictory since Absolute Being already excludes Absolute Nonbeing. When Lynch discusses finite entities, however, he will refer to *relative* being and *relative* nonbeing. In finite entities, relative being and relative nonbeing are contraries. Relative nonbeing merely describes the fact that any created entity is finite. It has limits. It does not exhaust what it means "to be" because other things "are" too. Any relative being will, therefore, also have as a contrary relative nonbeing. God must be the source of this nonbeing, which God produces in order to make an "other." This is possible because God's oneness is already an infinity, an unlimited, a freedom, and not simply a monolithic one. Thus, infinity makes God "splitable," or able to have an "other." In a sense, the infinite in God does not describe only a negative attribute. It also describes the positive ability to create an "other."

This ability to make others does not, however, destroy the oneness of God. Perhaps, in an analogous way, we might say that God's oneness is enhanced through its expression in others. God's "one" does not compete with God's "other," but grants the "other"

---

14. Rudolf Otto, *The Idea of the Holy: An Inquiry into the Non-rational Factor in the Idea of the Divine and Its Relation to the Rational*, trans. J. Harvey (New York: Oxford University Press, 1978), 26, 29-30.

an identity. We need to be related to our "One" as fully as possible to achieve our most authentic identity. An analogy of the two levels of consideration may be seen in the musical composer, Aaron Copland. At the first level of consideration, Copland himself is a "one" and a "many." He is a person with identifiable parts (e.g., organs, limbs, a certain sensibility, a psychological makeup, etc.) that can be considered as "others" that participate in the unity that is Aaron Copland. Although this Copland can be divided in an analytical sense, he cannot be multiplied. There can never again be another Aaron Copland. When God is considered as Absolute Being, God too is a one and an infinite, but not in a sense that we can divide or multiply.

There is another way of considering God. God's relation to creation might be compared to a composer and his or her composition. Suppose Copland composes music such as his *Appalachian Spring*. That ballet music may be identified as an "other" of Aaron Copland. It is another form of the "many" that participates in Copland. If the opening note of that ballet stood all alone, it would be the "other" of only the instrument that struck the note. However, if the rest of the ballet follows, that note takes on a fullness of character that it could not possibly achieve by itself. Heard in the context of the entire ballet, it becomes part of Copland's "other." Being part of a whole does not diminish the note. It enhances it.[15] This second level of consideration describes God and creation. Creation is God's freely chosen "other." It achieves its fullness only by being related to the One who created it. The "other" gains nothing by an attempt to assert itself as an individual apart from the "One" who grants it an identity. It would be like a note seeking to be the other of only the instrument that sounded it.

Furthermore, one might imagine Copland "losing himself," or perhaps better, "identifying himself," in the music at an actual performance of *Appalachian Spring*. An exhilarating integration of composer and work might ensue. Here the "one" does not become diminished through his "other." To the contrary, he finds

---

15. It might also help to think of the one that is augmented by its other in terms of motherhood. Even though the mother has given birth to an "other," that generative process does not compromise her "oneness." It enhances it.

himself in the "other." As Copland finds himself in his musical creation, *Appalachian Spring,* might not God find an analogous other in creation – a real Appalachian spring?[16]

It follows that when a "one" produces an "other," the active dynamic between the "one" and the "other" produces an augmentation of reality. In a sense, the "other" is at a distance from the "one," but the "one" nevertheless remains at hand, giving the other its very existence. God and humanity do not occupy the same distance from each other. While this might not make geometric sense, it does make ontological sense. For example, considered in terms of the bonds of personal relationship, a mother is closer to her baby than her baby is to her. This position supports the Augustinian dictum that God is closer to us than we are to ourselves. In describing God as the "Infinite-One," and ourselves (indeed, all of creation) as the "many," a panentheistic position is adopted. We might say that God is manifested in the moment of interpenetration of the finite and infinite. That continuous moment is called "creation," and it shares in both the freedom and the definiteness of God. It is a creation that eventually becomes self-conscious. Creation is the symphony of God. It is God's offspring, God's "other." It reaches its high point, the moment of perfect interpenetration of the infinite and finite, in Jesus Christ.

In addition, if we are God's "other," God's "many," then we should treat our relationship to our "One" as a relationship precisely as a "we," a "many," who are unified to our "one" who gives us existence. Our most profound moment of unity does not come from a superficial attempt to look like each other, but it comes from our relationship to the "One" who is God. While there is a legitimate value in each individual person, that value is not

16. It would be interesting to reflect on some other possibilities that this metaphor contains. For example, consider the following comments by Copland: "There have been instances when I have listened to performances of my work and thought: this is all very fine, but I don't think I recognize myself. . . . And similarly, it is from the finest interpreters that the composer can learn most about the character of his work; aspects of it that he did not realize were there. . . ." Aaron Copland, *Music and Imagination* (Cambridge: Harvard University Press, 1977), 17. Might those comments describe analogously certain aspects of the relationship between God and creation?

attained in a solipsistic way. Rather, the individual has a setting, a context, called "we." Hence, the oneness of God is reflected in the finite world through the determined, particular "ones" we encounter everyday in a unity that gives shape and meaning to its members. Those "ones" gain their existence ultimately from participating in the oneness of God. The infinity of God is reflected in the indeterminate, in the indefinite aspect of the finite, in our inwardness, in the spiritual. Both one and many, infinite and finite, natural and supernatural are distinguishable for us, but not separable.

As experienced within the finite nature of a human being, the infinite or the sacred "is par excellence the inner life, the absolute self-possession and self-identity of God."[17] The sacred is marked by "internality" or "selfhood."[18] Lynch also described the infinite as "meaning to the full," which is realized within "pure, unalloyed, concrete objects."[19] It is the grace of inwardness. On the other hand, the "outward," the concrete individual who experiences the inner life, constitutes the finite. It seems to be the analogue of the oneness of God. Both "inside" and "outside" depend on God for their existence and for their unity. The task is to share the inwardness and identity of God through each one's concrete outward nature. If the "Infinite-One" is truly a constitutive aspect of the finite, then there is no need to go beyond the finite, limited Christ to arrive at infinite "meaning, joy or illumination."[20]

Throughout his discussion of the relationship of the one and the many, Lynch is in effect discussing his doctrine of grace. Grace and nature are not contraries. Rather, grace designates the appropriate relationship between two terms that *are* contraries: the natural and the supernatural. Grace describes the dynamic relationship between the One and the many, God and creation,

---

17. William F. Lynch, *Christ and Prometheus: A New Image of the Secular* (Notre Dame: University of Notre Dame Press, 1970), 130. Hereinafter cited as "*CP*."

18. William F. Lynch, "Toward a Theology of the Secular," *Thought* 41, no. 162 (Autumn 1966): 364.

19. *CA* 15.

20. Ibid.

the divine and the human. Too often some religionists have tended to speak of grace and nature as if *they* were the contraries.

Grace has no contrary. But it does have a contradictory. The contradictory of grace is sin. Sin describes the disordered relationship between the One and the many, the natural and the supernatural, God and creation. Sin is analogous to the attempt of the many to organize the whole. An attempt is made to fashion an individual identity apart from the intelligibility of the Whole. It is rebellion from the One. Here people no longer wish to be the other of the One, but to be only their own. In sin, people are content to be a sheer many.

Reality for Lynch is filled with contraries, but those contraries are meant to be at home with each other. Reality is "dipolar," but not "conflictual."[21] It is meant to be wholesome. There is to be a positive, creative interplay among the contraries contained within any being. Indeed, all existents are relational to each other.[22] The infinite penetrates the finite, and, in a creative interplay with it, produces new possibilities of inwardness and self-possession. Reality, therefore, is not stagnant. It changes. It becomes richer in the dialectic. To the extent that one term attempts to destroy the other, a loss is suffered.[23]

From these observations, Lynch is in a position to propose that all existents possess an analogical structure. All beings are composed entities that participate in both being and relative non-being. They are analogical in that they contain the same and the different within their very structure. By virtue of their "double

---

21. *IH* 229ff. Lynch, "Death as Nothingness," *Continuum* 5, no. 3 (autumn 1967): 468.

22. *CP* 137; *IH* 151-52.

23. Such destruction is possible when, for instance, the absolute is viewed as a mechanical force residing outside the human. If the absolute does not partake of the relative in a positive interplay, then it may easily be considered as "foreign" or inimical to the concrete. Such an absolute would be seen as a dictator whose rules may be decreed quite apart from the needs and capabilities of its relative finite counterparts. However, when the absolute is seen as that which enables one to develop a personal interiority, to establish an identity, to form a wish, then the absolute has become a welcome collaborator in the human project. Indeed, the absolute enables us to become what we are at our best. *IH* 229ff.; id., "Theology of the Secular," 363-64.

participation," Lynch saw that things not only have their own reality in their own right but also participate in the larger community of being. On the other hand, concrete existents are also unique. As each act of existence expresses itself in this or that thing, it is always a new act of existence expressing itself according to a certain degree of possibility. Existence ". . . descends analogously, *ana-logon*, 'according to a proportion.'" That particular mouse, Lynch reminds us, has not existed previous to its life. The mouse can perceive and express only so much of what it means to be. It is a limited analogy of being. Its limitation (what it is not, or its quality of being "different") is found right in the heart of what it is as a mouse. So too each human being represents a new act of existence. As Lynch notes, the problem is that we do not quite know how much relative "being" a human person can handle in the midst of his or her relative "non-being."[24]

The temptation, of course, is to become impatient with analogy, and to separate the relative "being" from the relative "non-being." Such a division produces a Gnostic dualism. Some would look for an "irreducible image" of being that would enable them to look at a finite entity and call it either all light or all darkness. This is not to say that there are no contradictories that cannot be reconciled (such as goodness and evil), but contraries are not contradictories.[25] With an analogical structure, there is no univocal core to being, no one image, no single point of attack, that includes all the complexities and contraries that life itself contains.[26] The analogical image attempts to hold together in proper proportion the various components that make up the reality imagined.

Thus, Lynch explicitly rejected an integralism that views truth as having "fallen from heaven" in a convenient system of logically interlocked univocal propositions. Such a conception is deficient since it keeps "ourselves unspotted from this world. . . ."[27] Reality fits together, but not according to the

---

24. *IM* 111, 115; *CA* 149, emphasis found in the original.
25. *IM* 102-5; *IH* 229ff.; *IM* 55.
26. Lynch, "Theology and the Imagination," 76-77.

univocal logic of integralists. The more complex Platonic logic is required. Finite and infinite are not merely juxtaposed as if the finite, complete unto itself, received an additional gift, the infinite, to enhance its existence. The relationship is more like the fish in water that derives its oxygen from the water itself. The water and oxygen are distinct but not separate. The water needs the oxygen structurally to be what it is. The finite is not a jumping-off point that enables us to get to the infinite. To the extent that we attempt to leave the finite, we are like fish out of water. Hence, Lynch would urge that we think in terms of "both-and," not "either-or."[28]

B. Epistemological Considerations

In Lynch's view, when a person comes to know any particular entity, that knowledge is, like the entity itself, analogous and dialectical. It is both the same as and different from the thing known. It is the same as the thing known because the knower is already situated in reality and already participates in the analogous interplay of the being and non-being that must take place within every actual entity. It is different from the thing known because the object participates in being according to its own Idea, according to its own proportionality.[29]

In order to know the more profound truths of existence, a person must be trained to perceive the interplay of contraries at work in all being. Otherwise, a sort of simplistic, static conception of flat "immutable, celestial truth" can result and can stifle the knower's appreciation of its complexity.[30] But once people become comfortable with the rich dialectic at work within different types of being – scientific, mathematical, artistic – they will be able to recognize the same activity at work in other fields of knowledge as well. They will be able to "catch on" to insights by a sort of connaturality through which they can recognize a quality by simply being in tune with it. It is recognition from the inside. Lynch cites Thomas Aquinas in noting that the thinking subject

---

27. *IM* 54.
28. *CA* 76; *IM* v.
29. *CA* 150-51.
30. *CA* 48.

actually confronts reality, but that the object is always known in terms of the subject. In other words, no one simply drinks in pure experience and calls it knowledge as if an object were grasped without a particular perspective. The mind is not a mirror.[31]

Furthermore, the subject comes to self-awareness through knowledge of others. Consciousness emerges as self-awareness in the presence of others. Thus, knowledge is a unitive act in which objects do not simply remain external challenges to the knower, but become part of the knower's own existence. They become part of the knower's world. Lynch calls them "the incarnated enlargement of his own being."[32] Hence, activities like art can be seen as an act of both knowledge and self-awareness. The work of art, for Lynch, never simply speaks on its own. It also speaks for its author.

Knowledge is never merely a separated piece of information. Because knowledge is an activity performed by a person, knowledge emerges as a total personal system consisting of "concrete perception, moral action, artistic creation, and insertion into society."[33] That is, knowledge is an activity of the good, the beautiful, the scientific, and the cultural. Thus, the moral person attains a sort of knowledge that the immoral person does not grasp. Those quickened by the beauty of things know more deeply than those with a duller aesthetical sense. The scientist who is adept at abstraction and analysis also penetrates a level of reality denied to those who cannot appreciate such operations. Those who are in tune with the myths, needs, capabilities, and values of their society also know reality in a deeper way than those who ignore those dimensions. It is interesting that Lynch also explored admiration as a way of knowing.[34] The one who

---

31. Idem, "The Problem of Freedom," 6; *IM* 116; *CP* 117. Much of the following discussion will probably unnerve poststructuralists. While important insights have been proposed by the likes of Jacques Derrida and others, that brand of philosophy seems to be still under construction. Recent important correctives have been proposed by John Searle in *The Construction of Social Reality* (New York: Free Press, 1995) 159-60. Searle reports that Derrida has accepted at least one important corrective in J. Derrida, *Limited, Inc.* (Evanston, Ill.: Northwestern University Press, 1988), 136.

32. *IM* 117.

33. Ibid.

can admire or revere the object in question knows more about that object than the one who does not have that sense of wonder.

It follows that the objective of knowledge is the truth of life as it is lived in relation to this world, as it changes, and as its people experience new situations, challenges, questions, and perspectives that are analogous to former times, but never simply the same.[35] As we will see, people not only perceive this world, they make it, and, therefore, bear some responsibility for it. The integralist perspective is found to be wanting on this score, and, in a sense, is guilty of refusing to recognize responsibility for the positive creation of the world in which we live.

Through Lynch's work, it can be seen that the modern "turn to the subject" is also a "turn to the world." Lynch specifically rejected the solipsistic turn toward the self. The turn to the "inside" is not to exclude the "outside." It is thus not opposed to the older notion of truth as adequation, or correspondence. It is rather its enrichment that enables us to turn more authentically to the world, and discover the profound riches of the finite.

II. Lynch's Method

A. The Analogical Imagination

If knowledge is dialectical, analogous, and personal, the tools by which one gains that knowledge should reflect those qualities. Lynch's basic tool for achieving reliable knowledge is the analogical imagination because it reflects those very qualities. First, the imagination will be considered, and then the qualities that make its images "analogical" will be inspected.

The imagination, for Lynch, is not a separate faculty such as the intellect or the will. Rather, it simply describes the activity whereby people make images. Such an activity is so wide-ranging that it becomes apparent that the imagination draws on all of the faculties, feelings, experiences, and life histories of those who

---

34. William F. Lynch, "In Admiration of Teilhard," *America* 132 (April 12, 1975): 274.
35. *IH* 193.

imagine. Lynch formulated the following description of the imagination:

> It is not a single or special faculty. It is all the resources of man, all his faculties, his whole history, his whole life, and his whole heritage, all brought to bear upon the concrete world inside and outside of himself, to form images of the world, and thus to find it, cope with it, shape it, even make it. The task of the imagination is to imagine the real. However, that might also very well mean making the real, making the world, for every image formed by everybody is an active step, for good or for bad.[36]

The concrete world is thus mediated to the person through the imagination, which, if it operates well, provides images that grant a certain "thickness" to reality. By "thickness," Lynch means that many dimensions should be brought together and kept together in one image. Images should be analogical in the sense that they preserve the various aspects of a reality in their proper proportion, especially its contraries. If an image highlights one dimension, it had better present that dimension as related to other dimensions in the thing imagined. It should never present one pole of a contrary relationship as if it could subsist on its own.[37] For example, while one might develop wonderful images of the Interior Castle of one's spiritual life, those images cannot be treated as if they could exist without one's Exterior Castle.

There is a transcendental imagination that allows us to see more than meets the eye. We synthesize both the side of the mountain that is in plain view and the side that is hidden. Furthermore, Lynch noted that there is a certain "freedom" of imagination that carries the realities we encounter to every nook and cranny of the human, and translates those realities into its own image. The imagination is not free when it becomes fixated on only one element of the reality imagined. For example, when the

---

36. *CP* 23. Lynch acknowledged Martin Buber for the insight that the task of the imagination is to imagine the real.

37. William F. Lynch, "Theology and the Imagination," *Thought* 29, no. 112 (Spring 1954): 66.

imagination becomes fascinated with sex or violence, Lynch noted that it was in a rut. It was imprisoned and it needed freeing.[38] With a conclusion reminiscent of Coleridge's esemplastic power of the imagination, Lynch asserted, "Thus ideally, no part of us is allowed to die or shrivel up or be cut off and imprisoned. It is not only allowed to speak, but to speak in its own language."[39]

By virtue of the imagination, things can also be presented with a certain depth. The imagination produces things as a synthesis of both meaning and presence. It does not merely reproduce things as "bare facts." The imagination creates new perspectives for the facts it has found. It gives them a "background," a "landscape." It presents the world as related to the human, as touched by the heart and mind. A newborn baby may be considered as a gift from God, but a different kind of imagination might see the baby differently, perhaps only as a burden. The baby is most likely both gift and burden. Nevertheless, that burden is gladly carried by those whose imaginations are adept at fashioning images of grace. The imagination is particularly well suited to form a pathway to reality because it can keep opposites together in a thought-provoking analogy or in a metaphor packed with new insight, or in a masterfully constructed story. Such operations of the imagination constitute real ontological reachings into our world.[40]

Such is true of the analogical imagination because it not only retains but it also displays the contraries that make up the very heart of any real entity we encounter. Since a being always exists "according to a measure," as something, as a particular mixture of being and non-being, as the same and yet different, our knowledge of that being reliable to the extent those opposites are kept "interlocked in one imaginative act."[41] Moreover, the analogical

38. William F. Lynch, *The Image Industries* (New York: Sheed and Ward, 1959), 72. Hereinafter cited as "*II*."

39. William F. Lynch, "The Task of Enlargement," *Thought* 51, no. 203 (December 1976): 246-349; 350. "Esemplastic" describes imagination's ability to produce a mutually effective interpenetration of the faculties. For example, by virtue of the esemplastic power of the imagination, the intellect can "understand" the emotions, even though the person's emotions do not produce concepts. See Appendix I, pp. 164-68.

40. *IH* 193-94, 248-49, 244.

41. *CA* 133.

imagination "moves with every change in reality. . . . It does not try to impose one single form of its own upon the world."[42] In other words, the analogical imagination is sensitive to the varying ways in which entities may be received into the world. For example, the analogical imagination will enable a society to shift its image of femininity according to the various ways that real women come to express their humanity.

Of course, it is apparent that, although images have an ontological value, they also can misguide the unwary. After all, there are plenty of images that are not simply contrary but contradictory. There are unrealistic images that compete for our attention and may lead to our doom. If the analogical imagination is to be a useful tool, its relationship to reason must be explored, and guidelines for making healthy images and recognizing poor images need to be developed.

In dealing with the rational, Lynch insists that thought and image belong together. The dichotomy between words and images introduces a false dualism that can encourage people to turn solely to concepts in their search for the real, or solely to images. As a consequence of such dualism, theologians may err in either of two ways – first, by assuming that images and culture hardly matter at all; and second, by assuming that the conceptually oriented theologian must go hat in hand to those who produce the images in society and accept their direction.[43]

Images provide more than mere ornamentation. Images embody thought. Images are compact with cognition, truth, and knowledge. Put simply, images think. They possess a cognitive value that is only dimly perceived at first. As the image is incorporated into the person's operating view of reality, that image, if it is a good one, will unfold deeper and deeper aspects

---

42. William F. Lynch, "Foundation Stones for Collaboration Between Religion and the Literary Imagination," *Journal of the American Academy of Religion* 47, no. 2, Supplement (June 1979): 343.

43. William F. Lynch, "Counterrevolution in the Movies," *Commonweal* 87 (October 20, 1967): 77; William F. Lynch, "The Life of Faith and Imagination: Theological Reflection in Art and Literature," *Thought* 57, no. 224 (March 1982): 13-14. For a discussion on the relationship between faith, images and rationality, see Chapter Three, Section III (C) below.

of the real. Once an appropriate image arises within a person's imagination, the image itself will unfold its meaning on several levels, including the ontological, the emotional, and the intellectual. The richer the analogy or metaphor, the richer its yield.[44]

Furthermore, we bear some responsibility for our images because we do not merely discover analogies, we create them. We also do not merely love or hate images, but the images themselves love or hate within us.[45] As we commit ourselves to an image, we begin to love what the image loves and hate what the image hates even though the full range of those objects of love and hatred remains somewhat hidden from view. Thus, for example, if a person chooses the myths surrounding the Nazi doctrine of Aryan supremacy, the person may be surprised to discover a self-hatred one day welling up within the heart. Alternatively, if one accepts the symbolic power of the cross, the life of faith can unfold in even more surprising ways. Finally, if one chooses both images simultaneously, one has chosen internal warfare.

The task of the imagination is to imagine the real. Its function is to keep the intelligence in touch with reality, "to prevent the mind from leaping into unearned insights or into a charlatanism of exploding ideas that do not have the human right or evidence for such explosions."[46] The imagination gives our concepts justification. It roots them in the real. Given a set of false images, the rational will yield a set of false conclusions. Conceptual thought can never be considered the only way to think. Such a position results from misplaced faith in Cartesian dualism. Conceptual thought investigates many things – logical operations, abstraction, classification, coherence, necessary assumptions, implications, etc. Lynch asserts, however, that thought "is mainly a struggle for right images." Lynch proposed that analogies attract

---

44. Lynch, "The Life of Faith and Imagination," 12, 9, 16; "Foundation Stones," 335. Paul Ricoeur's philosophy is somewhat different, since it seems that thought is extrinsic to the symbol. The thought for Ricoeur takes place somewhere else: "The symbol, in effect, only gives rise to thought if it first gives rise to speech." See *IT* 55.

45. Lynch, "Theology of Faith and Imagination," 16.

46. Lynch, "A Dramatic Making of the Human," *Humanitas* 14, no. 2 (May 1978): 170.

our attention primarily because of their positive content. They are used because of what they say, not because of what they leave unsaid. Stating that "God is more real than this iron bar" informs our minds in a positive direction. If we conceive that the iron bar is real, so much the more ought we to conceive of God as real.[47]

Thought and image are mutually supportive and mutually critical. If a poor image is proposed, conceptual thought may assist in illustrating its shortcomings. In that case, the search for a new image or a supplementary image may continue. Paul Ricoeur illustrates such a rational process in his *Symbolism of Evil,* in which he shows how evil is such a thick, elusive reality that it requires several images to convey its meaning. The rational must be used as one of the tools that sorts through the various images to discover their bases and implications.

On the other hand, poor theory may be critiqued by a telling image. Through the action (drama) of the imagination, our rational, predictable, rather neat, theoretically constructed world meets the "diffusion" and "diffraction" of reality. Lynch's theory of diffusion proposes that once an action is posited in the real world, it meets a certain resistance, and can never "remain itself." Alternatively, one may think of it as diffraction "because under the weight of the world it diffracts and breaks up" somewhat as a beam of light breaks apart as it passes through a prism.[48] Allow the best laid plans to begin to take shape. Once they hit the prism of reality, they oftentimes break into such varied and unantici-pated pieces that immediately adjustments must be made:

> It becomes an adventure. Now only the imagination can take over its course. More often everything goes ordinar-ily, with the usual diffraction of an idea as it enters the world, as enter it must. But almost as often it does not. The message of Romeo to Juliet enters crookedly and tardily; we should not say that it does not get there, it does not get there as intended by some pure and loving intelligence, but gets there late and madly. The original

---

47. Lynch, "Foundation Stones," 335; id., "The Imagination of the Drama," *Review of Existential Psychology and Psychiatry* 14, no. 1 (1975-76): 2. Lynch, "Death as Nothingness," 467. Lynch, "Images of Faith," 192.

48. Lynch, "The Imagination of the Drama," 3-4.

word or event becomes splashes of fragmentation or sorrow, diverted from its pure lines and intentions by the rougher lines of the people in between the pure idea and the world.[49]

Lacking the benefit of dramatic diffraction, the imageless thought can be just as false as the thoughtless image. Both the logic of the rational and the diffraction of the dramatic must be brought to bear on the various ways we deal with reality – whether we consider it by thought or by image. The two should not be treated as if they can be separated.

In spite of the dialectical interplay of thought and image, still the desire for a rational proof persists. The mind yearns for a way to "prove" that one image is true to life, and another is false. In only a highly analogous sense, can we speak of such a thing as proof. The difficulty is that "proof" deals with only a segment of reality: that segment that can be manipulated externally. Lynch notes that the *ratio* deals with external relations, while the imagination deals with internal relations.[50] Hence, a peculiar type of "proof" may exist, but not in an extrinsic sort of way whereby our grasp of one thing assures us that another must follow. The very question is, Are we grasping this thing, or do we have really another, perhaps an illusion?

Lynch asserts that the imagination is the very process of proof. The way something is imagined will create either problems or solutions. As questions begin to vanish and partners to the dialogue are satisfied, a sort of "proof" will be attained. When something is successfully imagined, we simply know. We understand the rationality embodied in that image. In a sense, the image is proof by connaturality. When the image is adequate, there is no need of further proof of its desirability.[51] Obviously, new questions and problems will emerge, but we will no longer be at the same point of discussion. For example, in *The Republic*, Plato's

---

49. Ibid., 4.
50. *CA* 123.
51. Lynch, "Foundation Stones," 335, 339; id., *Images of Faith: An Exploration of the Ironic Imagination* (Notre Dame: University of Notre Dame Press, 1973), 3. Hereinafter cited as "*IF*."

discussion on the nature of justice concluded because every party to the dialogue was satisfied. No one had any further questions in view of the image of justice Plato had fashioned. It is that sort of "proof" that the imagination can produce.

If imagination itself constitutes the proof that we are in touch with reality, we need to consider various ways the imagination is used and misused, and from that perspective, bolster some of the controls we have in employing the imagination as a method in theology. One of the most important qualities that supports the healthy imagination is a lively sensibility. By sensibility, Lynch meant the ability appropriately to shift one's feelings and reactions according to the reality that is being encountered at the moment. Its first movements must be marked by "concern and knowledge." Then, as new phases are encountered, the imagination must move and shift accordingly.[52] Our images carry much of our encounter with reality, including its emotional tone. Sensibility preserves the human dimension of feelings. Reaction to people and things should vary according to many factors. Sorrow is appropriate at some points but not at others. The images that grow from our sensible contact with reality need to be as rich and varied as our human sensibility.

A certain sense of both seriousness and parody should constitute the salt and pepper of the imagination that keeps a lively sensibility intact. Otherwise the imagination becomes fixated, paralyzed, and desperate. The fixated imagination will break out in indirect forms of the monstrous. Eventually, an ersatz form of the imagination takes over, and it generates images of the violent or the pornographic. For example, as balanced images of sexuality or death are suppressed, the imagination no longer holds opposites together. Then, Lynch observes, "The fear and insecurity that comes from a lack of coping-by-imagining leads to every manner of *solving-by-attacking*."[53]

---

52. William F. Lynch, "The Bacchae of Euripides: An American Parallel," *New York Images* no. 3 (autumn 1986): 21-22; id., "What's Wrong with 'Equus'? Ask Euripides," *America* 133 (December, 1975): 421; *IM* 131; id., "The Problem of Freedom," 15; id., "Counterrevolution in the Movies," 79; id., "Euripides' 'Bacchae': The Mind in Prison," *Cross Currents* 25 (summer 1975): 168.

53. Lynch, "Death as Nothingness," 460; id., "The Bacchae of Euripides," 22.

When the imagination fails to maintain the tensive analogous quality of reality, it focuses on one aspect and invests that aspect with absolute value. That failure of the imagination constitutes the "absolutizing instinct" that enables a person to fantasize. In this movement, which contradicts Plato's dictum that the whole gives meaning to the parts, whatever part is wished as an absolute is hunted down, and, wherever it is found, it is allowed to give meaning to the whole. Absolutizers are quick to fashion idols out of their needs: money, companionship, power, knowledge, reassurance, etc. For example, the star-crossed lover beholds his love and declares her to be Love itself. Regardless of the actual mixture of good and bad that she really is, he falls in love with his fantasy instead.[54]

A corrective for the absolutizing instinct can be found in "enlargement." When a person's view of reality has become fixed on one aspect, the imagination should be able to furnish the greater context in which that absolutized element can be situated. It should be able to furnish the landscape that can bring the proper perspective to relativize the portion of reality that has been given disproportionate weight. The view should be enlarged to the point where the contrary can once again be seen in its dialectical role. For example, when the task of enlargement has been performed well, the person moves beyond the position of tolerance in which a person merely recognizes that other people see things differently. The healthy, analogical imagination attempts to keep diverse relative viewpoints together, acknowledging the extent to which each relative viewpoint is true. In that way, one could hardly absolutize one's own relative position.[55]

---

54. *IH* 113, 105-107.
55. *IH* 244, 249. It is also helpful to note that when a person has absolutized an element of reality that causes pain, the enlargement of that pain's context into its total framework – including its historical, social, and theological settings – begins to reduce the inordinate claim that the particular disturbance had when it was allowed to occupy the status of an absolute. While contextualization may not slay the monster, it does help to see that the offending element of reality is not quite as monstrous as we had supposed.

The absolutizing instinct also plays a decisive role in the polarizing or Gnostic imagination. This type of imagination depends on the Cartesian ability to abstract and separate the relevant qualities, no matter how tightly bound together they are in reality. Issues can then be simplified in terms of "pro" and "con" without ever recognizing that there can be more than two sides to an issue. If the imagination insists on viewing reality in "pure" terms, that is, without grappling with the ambiguities and tensions of a dipolar reality, then it will give rise to the "equivocal mind." Such can happen when we compartmentalize specialties. A poet might claim that a given poem does not include a psychological or a theological position. Such a poet would suppose that the literary imagination has nothing to do with the theological imagination. For example, those plagued by the equivocal imagination would consider it possible to come before God and to stand as an individual person but not also as a member of a specific society.[56]

If the equivocal imagination sees everything as different, the univocal imagination distorts reality by seeing everything as the same. The univocal mind attempts to lead a simple and clear intellectual life. Words like "love," "prayer," and "one" have only a single meaning. In its "ascending mode," the univocal mind uses a term in exactly the same sense for all its subjects. It requires a process of abstraction that sets aside and ignores the differences. Perfect theoretical unity is reached. Even though univocity is a necessary concern for the scientific mind, problems can occur when we attempt to leave the abstract and reenter the realm of concrete reality without returning to an analogical way of thinking. For example, the concept of marriage will achieve such levels of abstraction that it will simply mean the same thing regardless of whether a couple happens to be newlyweds or great-grandparents. An analogical mind would be open to pertinent differences and would allow a richer notion of marriage to breathe life into the resulting concept.

In its "descending mode," the univocal mind attempts "to shape the real . . . according to its own forms and single-minded passions." It now enters the world of action and attempts to flatten

---

56. *IH* 160-61; *IF* 72; *CA* 163-65.

everything according to its own categories and "eliminate the unlike, the different, the pluralistic, as a kind of intractable and even hostile material."[57] In its descending mode, the univocal mind is often expressed in actions rooted in the prejudices of the day. It results in unfortunate encounters like the one expressed in Ralph Ellison's *Invisible Man*: "I am invisible, understand, simply because people refuse to see me. . . . When they approach me they see only my surroundings, themselves, or figments of their imagination – indeed, everything and anything except me."[58]

Lynch proposed his doctrine of "emergence" as the way in which a healthy imagination approaches reality. By emergence, Lynch means simply that any entity, any "one," ought to be allowed to speak for itself. It need not go outside itself to establish its value or nature. No preestablished thought system ought to be allowed to dictate the parts that go into its makeup, or what it ought to look like at maturity. By emergence, a thing comes into its own identity by which it "can be located in itself and distinguished from everything else." If the Gnostic imagination destroys the identity of a thing by separating its parts, a healthy analogical imagination grants the thing its proper autonomy. It will be able "to articulate the parts and jointings of that which it beholds" as the imagination is embodied in language. More sensitive and intelligent dealings with reality ought to ensue.[59]

The doctrine of emergence also respects the analogical as that which is new. The analogical imagination listens to a reality rather than either dismissing it as simply another instance of the same thing we all have seen before, or dismissing it as so unique that it has no connection with anything else. So, for example,

---

57. *CA* 114-16, 117-18.
58. Ralph Ellison, *Invisible Man* (New York: Random House, 1952), 3.
59. *CP* 129; id., "Theology of the Secular," 351. *IF* 67-68. An example of the univocal imagination that fails to allow emergence to operate can be seen in the melting pot image that dominated the liberal thinking of the Americanists around the end of the nineteenth century. As the waves of immigrants settled in various ethnic communities, many were asked to "Americanize" their ways by giving up their original customary ways of dancing, singing, educating their young, and practicing Catholic devotions. Rather than allowing a real unity to emerge from such cultural diversity, an artificial uniformity was often imposed. "Theology of the Secular," 352-53.

when we encounter a grieving man, we ought never to presume that "we know exactly how you feel." That man's grief is analogical. It is a new instance of grief in this world. We may have a notion of what grief is like in general, but this man's grief is a particular instance of grief that calls for our attentiveness. We must let it emerge on its own terms, and, if we receive this person's grief with an analogical imagination, we will learn something new about what it means to grieve. The analogical imagination at this fundamental level is not so much concerned with distinguishing the same and the different as it is concerned with preventing a univocal imagination from taking charge as if it already knew what was the same (our general notion of grief) and what was different (merely another person experiencing the same old feelings of loss that everyone has had, albeit in different circumstances). The analogical imagination allows the new to emerge on its own terms in its own way. It is free to fashion new images that will allow this particular instance of grief to speak for itself, and, thereby, to put us in touch with a new experience of this human dimension that can arise within our human community.[60]

B. Drama as Method

Since knowledge is discovered through action for Lynch, it makes sense for him to use action ($\alpha\rho\alpha m\alpha$ =*drama*) as a tool to further our knowledge. As such, the literary process offers a convenient vehicle because it constitutes a "highly cognitive passage through the finite and definite realities of man and the world." In other words, drama and literature offer us the opportunity to view the diffraction of our theories about life as those theories might enter reality. The theologian needs assurance that his thought is rooted in reality, and also the benefit of the heuristic value of seeing the play bring a theory of life in collision with circumstances that perhaps were not envisioned in the original theory.[61]

---

60. *CA* 148-52.
61. *CA* xi; "Foundation Stones," 338.

Of course, a play usually does not, and should not, begin in didactic fashion with an explanation of a theory that is about to be tested. But, as a play proceeds, its underlying values and theories – its point of view – will emerge. But then the playwright can let the action take sudden, unexpected turns in such a way that we find ourselves reforming our original images. With that reformation of images comes an implicit critique of earlier theories, and a possible way those theories may be reformulated. The talented playwright can "force us" to "re-cognize" reality. Thus, Aeschylus, in his play *The Persians*, written soon after the Greeks had defeated the Persian empire in 480 B.C., required his audience to see through the usual facilely constructed categories of victor and vanquished. Through his artistry, the audience was invited to re-cognize its idea of the human so as to see that not only "Greek" but also "Persian" is also a way of being human. The more Persian, the more human. In such a conversion of images, the analogical imagination is refreshed because the dialectical tension of being and nonbeing is once again brought back into play.[62]

That sort of "re-cognizing" activity reflects the doctrine of "recollection" of Plato. The knowledge given by a good teacher does not impose itself from the outside. There is a certain knowledge from the inside. "Recollection" seeks to awaken a sense for the analogical aspect of being in which everyone is already situated albeit unconsciously. As students become comfortable with the fact that things can be the same, yet different, they will accept teaching about reality "from the inside" as if recollecting something they already knew. Knowledge thus can be presented as "friendly" because it was already a part of their lives.[63]

Drama, for Lynch, constitutes a way to recollect, a way to "re-cognize" reality. It is a way to catch on to analogies that are yet inadequately perceived. The more adept we become in handling the analogical, the more reliable our knowledge will be. Of course, there can be bad drama just as there can be bad

---

62. *IF* 20; Idem, "A Dramatic Making," 165.
63. Lynch, "The Problem of Freedom," 105-6.

philosophy and bad theology. Lynch offers many examples of drama that fail because they are faithless to the concrete, finite dimensions of human existence. The more faithful drama is to the finite, the more fruitful will be its yield. For example, in tragedy we should be led to an awareness of the last moment of human finitude: thoroughgoing helplessness. At death all energy is gone. Through the tragic imagination, death is discovered, not as an ontic "fact" or as a statistic, but as the ultimate dimension of our reality as finite. Yet in that moment of finitude, if the playwright is talented, the audience will be able to detect the awesome dimension of the infinite. Lynch contends that such is the effect of the classic Greek and Shakespearean tragedies.[64]

However, there is a dishonest tragic imagination at work in much of the modern theater. It is characterized by a loss of nerve in its march through the finite circumstances of life. As it approaches the climax where all appears to be lost, a great reversal takes place. The result is a romantic, direct grasping for the infinite through an abandonment of the finite. The finite is used as a jumping off point to the infinite. Lynch offers, ". . . Ibsen, for example, with his rhetorical ending in *Enemy of the People* when Dr. Stockman is able to cry out in the midst of his pain, as Oedipus never could, 'The strongest man in the world is he who stands most alone.'" These "tragedies of a 'new dawn'" get people off the hook. The pain of the finite is not really pain at all. It is merely an opportunity through which the character can show that he or she is really infinite, immortal, and above it all. This "tragedy of defiance," while seductive in its artistry, yields a flattened distortion of reality through its failure to hold on to the finite pole of reality. It constitutes a play written from the top of the head, and not from the drama or action of life. Hence, Lynch observes, its popularity has remained largely confined to intellectuals. Lynch developed similar insights through a consideration of comedy. Good comedy has a way of exposing people's unwarranted pretensions. It celebrates the finite in "bringing us down to earth." As exemplified by such characters as Sancho Panza, comedy allows people to be simple and dignified in their own way.[65]

---

64. *CA* xi, 66, 67-68.

The artist should put people in touch with reality. That task demands a well-tuned sensibility to the human dimensions that are reflected in everyone's lives. The artist should not be set apart from the common folk. Lynch notes that the "the great artists explored the hearts of people for their materials and only differed from them finally in that they were able to say for men and women what the latter were not able to say for themselves." They are able to perceive the serious and the important, the tragic and the helpless, and theatrically move them to center stage where it will not hurt quite as much to look at them as it does in real life.[66]

Yet an element of the real needs to be kept in view. This function was quite literally served by the mountains and seas that formed the background of the ancient Greek amphitheaters. Drama is not to be a solipsistic affair showing us only the psychological bleeding of an individual apart from society and the world. Such an event, Lynch claims, would look puny in comparison to the mountains in the distance. The dramatic imagination should help us enter the greater arena of life. There should be a movement from a private to a public imagination. Take, for example, the *Medea* of Euripedes. Lynch asks us to imagine the speech of Jason, who, like a second-rate lawyer, attempts to assist Medea in rationalizing that his new marriage is all for the best. Lynch points out for us that:

> This speech *might* be able to hide itself in a small indoor theater. Among the mountains only Medea, for good or bad, is the measure of the mountains. Thus, the mountains can properly be imagined as leading the contemptuous laughter at the petty logic of Jason.[67]

On the other hand, as the noble spirit is revealed, the depths of the human seem to coincide with the towering mountains. As Roman theater began to erect its own artificial scenic structure that

---

65. *CA* 70, 73, 76, 91ff.

66. *IM* 133. William F. Lynch, "Easy Dramatic Lessons on . . . How to Miss Reality . . . How to Hit It," *Images of New York: A Journal of Places, Arts, Literature* no. 1 (spring 1984): 19.

67. William F. Lynch, "The Drama of the Mind: An Ontology of the Imagination," *Notre Dame English Journal: A Journal of Religion in Literature* 13, no. 1 (fall 1980): 25-26.

obscured the mountains and the seas, Lynch contends that plays began to express a more purely inward imagination. In such a play, the drama of the mind dominates to such an extent that the rest of the world "either does not exist or is destroyed." In putting us in touch with the real, the artist needs to employ and to excite within us a public imagination that enters into a dialectical exchange with that reality so that new perceptions of the world might become part of our conscious reality.[68]

Such a movement into new consciousness does not call for demythologization whereby myths are reduced to a set of concepts. Rather, the task is to remythologize in images that respond to our current experiences, problems, and concerns. To achieve such a lofty goal, current images often need to be "de-created" or "de-symbolized." Old worn-out symbols can deplete their value through overuse or misuse. They can obscure contraries that need to be recognized, or they can be overloaded with too much content and display aspects that are not really there. New efforts must be initiated to reach for symbols that will more effectively communicate reality to us. But first there must be a sort of "descent into hell" whereby we come to admit that our familiar symbols, so glibly placed that they are hardly noticed, were in collusion with us in providing comfort but not much reality. For example, some choose to see Christ in everyone while missing the beauty and value of the concrete person they have before their very eyes.[69]

The stripping process is the effort of a community. Neither the theologian alone nor the playwright alone can make it happen. But the artist does attempt a central task through drama. According to Aeschylus, he who acts must suffer and learn. The playwright's contribution starts with some action (*drama*) that meets the diffraction of unforeseen circumstances. That action then turns to suffering (παθος, *pathos*), until it reaches a new level of insight or point of reconciliation (Μαθος, *mathos*).[70]

---

68. Ibid., 26-27; id., "Foundation Stones," 339; id., "The Imagination of the Drama," 9.
69. *CP* 30, 47, 25-26.
70. Lynch, "The Imagination of Drama," 3; *CP* 24.

In the drama phase, an old hypothesis is played out. It passes through the finite domain of the human. As an example, Lynch uses Aeschylus' *Oresteia*. The drama concerns a type of *quid pro quo* justice that generates a chain of violence from one generation to the next. Each generation must vindicate the honor of their ancestors through a sort of "equalizing vengeance." This conception of justice produces a maddening, endless, hopeless future.[71]

At this point, the second phase, *pathos,* or the suffering of the passage to a new hypothesis, is portrayed. In a sense, *pathos* is the opposite of *drama. Drama* acts. *Pathos* passively suffers an action. This in-between state represents a time of normlessness and anomie. The old hypothesis no longer works, but it is the established, fixed way of doing things. The new is not yet in sight.[72] One can only suffer, trusting that the passage through one's finitude will eventually bear fruit. The positive gain here is that the imagination is freed from considering the old hypothesis as *the* definition of reality. The chief temptation during this phase is to abandon the imagination and fix things by an act of willful violence.[73]

In the final phase, *mathos,* a new hypothesis is discovered. There comes a moment of equity, wisdom and humanity that perceives a way to bring the endless to an end. At its best, Lynch notes that the new hypothesis includes the old, but goes beyond it. This sublative process occurs in our example when Orestes submits to a trial at the Areopagus. The votes for and against him are equal. It is Athena who casts the deciding vote to release him without exonerating him. Nor are the Furies banished. Freedom is affirmed, along with the reality and terror of justice. A new level of justice, "equity," has been reached. Humankind is now called to administer justice, to manage it, not simply to submit to its mechanical requirements. Justice mixed with mercy becomes a new possibility with a deeper, more analogical notion of justice in hand that now can become part of the custom of the city. But

---

71. *CP* 53, 77.

72. In a sense, this is a prolonged version of the "instant" described by Plato in *The Parmenides*. See Hypothesis IIa in Appendix II.

73. *CP* 81-82, 85-86.

this stage is not one of simply resolution. Any new stage brings the pangs of guilt along with it, and, consequently, an agonizing search for innocence follows.[74]

III. The Compass and the Quadrant Are One

As Ahab squinted at the sun, attempting to use his quadrant, the Parsee "was kneeling beneath him on the ship's deck, and, with face thrown up like Ahab's, was eyeing the same sun with him, only the lids of his eyes half hooded their orbs, and his wild face was subdued to an unearthly passionlessness."[75] Soon the Parsee would depend solely on the vertical for guidance, and Ahab solely on the horizontal – he one passionless, the other filled with rage. Both reach their goal, the White Whale, yet both were consumed by that goal.

That perhaps is the danger of the distorted imagination: it can reach its goal. The problem is that such a goal is an illusion. It can consume its pursuer either through a passionless fixation or through an uncontrolled rage. If one is to reach the full texture of reality, both horizontal and vertical need to be seen together because reality contains both together. Throughout this chapter, William Lynch has offered us tools to keep us on the path to reality. Lynch's methodological tools, like the compass and quadrant, do not provide a preset agenda or destination. They provide a continuing orientation without which there is no "destination" as such, but only a chance drifting.

The major tool Lynch provides, the analogical imagination, requires a lively sensibility, a willingness to learn from drama, a respect for emergence, a welcoming of the enlarged point of view, a willingness to resymbolize reality, and a resolve to attend to the concrete, finite dimensions of the real. In holding firm to these qualities, we hold firm to an instrument that keeps tune with both the natural and the supernatural, the horizontal and the vertical, the immanent and the transcendent. Indeed, in holding firm to

---

74. *CP* 91, 101ff.
75. Melville, *Moby Dick*, chap. 118, p. 609.

these qualities, we can develop the analogical habit that is comfortable in perceiving "both/and" relationships rather than the "either/or" separations that can throw us off course.

As we grapple with the real world and begin to perceive both the immanent and transcendent, the finite and infinite, we begin to understand that while there is a needed distinction between the horizontal and the vertical, their prior unity also needs to be kept in view. In gleaning the unity of those dimensions, we ought also to be aware that the instruments of theology need to reflect that unity. To destroy the instruments that show us the horizontal is to destroy the instruments that show us the vertical. In a sense, both compass and quadrant are one.

CHAPTER THREE

Faith as the
Ironic Christic Imagination

AS THE WOODEN PRISON DOOR FLUNG OPEN, A YOUNG WOMAN HOLDING her infant stepped out of the darkness into the harsh sunlight. Nathaniel Hawthorne described the most unusual feature of her dress:

> On the breast of her gown, in fine red cloth, surrounded with an elaborate embroidery and fantastic flourishes of gold thread, appeared the letter A. It was so artistically done, and with so much fertility and gorgeous luxuriance of fancy, that it had all the effect of a lasting and fitting decoration to the apparel she wore.[1]

This "fertile" letter fastened to the bodice of her dress was intended to expose the proud Hester Prynne to a raw form of shame as punishment for her adultery. As she ascended the scaffold to endure the disdain of the townsfolk, Hester instinctively held her baby close to her bosom. Hawthorne noted, ironically, "Had there been a Papist among the crowd of Puritans he might have seen in this beautiful woman . . . an object to remind him of the image of Divine Maternity."[2]

Accordingly, this figure of mother and child eventually became transfigured. Throughout the ensuing years, the towns-

---

1. Nathaniel Hawthorne, *The Scarlet Letter*, ed. S. Bradley et al, A Norton Critical Edition (New York: W. W. Norton, 1978), chap. 2, p. 43.
2. Ibid., p. 45.

folk observed Hester's dignified bearing, good works, and devotion to her anonymous love. Slowly, they began not to revile, but
to reverence both the letter and its wearer. Ironically, the A that
originally stood for "Adulteress" began to display its fertility in
being understood also as "Able," "Artist," "Angel," "Apostle,"
"Atonement," and "Affection." They called her "our Hester" and
looked upon her almost as a nun wearing the symbol of her order.
While modern writing is replete with images of the virgin who is
transformed into a whore, Hawthorne has given us precisely the
opposite movement: Hester, the Adulteress, has become the
Virgin. Even her little impish child, the offspring of sin, credited
by Hester herself with her salvation, could be seen briefly in the
role of the Christ child.

As these ironies unfold, Hawthorne seems to have given us
the story of the salvation of both Hester Prynne and the townsfolk
who knew her. It is the story of their simple, yet not so simple,
faith, for, as Lynch suggests, it is precisely faith that gives rise to
the way people look on this world, including its virgins and
children. Hester was saved not simply by her artistry in crafting
a letter so beautiful that it could call for people's attention and
admiration. She was saved also by the human and divine ability
to "see into" the A, and therefore to "see into" her. She and others
were saved by the ability of the scarlet letter to pry open the
sensibilities of a hardened people so that one soul might touch
another. She was saved by the grace through which it is possible
to imagine what had previously been unimaginable. Neither the
letter alone nor Hester alone could accomplish such a transformation. The combination of *this* person wearing *this* symbol in
this way, in *this* context, however, allowed the miracle to unfold.

So much is salvation connected with the way we treat
images, and, therefore, the people who must wear those images,
that Lynch asserts, "We shall be finally judged by our images as
much as by any other factor in the human condition. So full of
thought and choice and freedom are they. Or so empty that they
are inhuman."[3] Faith's images may either swing open a prison

---

3. Lynch, "The Life of Faith and Imagination," 11.

door or slam it shut. The effect of our images truly reveals the shape of the faith that produces those images.

Lynch considered faith to be the healthy operation of an ironic Christic imagination. In reviewing Lynch's approach to faith, we will first explore his treatment of faith as imagination. Then we will consider how such an image leads to salvation, explain its relationship to reason, and finally review its relationship to time as it unfolds in the course of a human life.

I. The Structure of Faith

A. The Imagination as Faith

Everyone needs an approach to reality. Some paradigm, some model, of the way reality unfolds in the life of any person is necessary for the person to have any coherent, intelligible experience. By "paradigm," Lynch means a pattern for understanding the experiences one has or the facts one encounters. A person cannot observe a fact without an expectation or without some hypothesis, in terms of which it makes sense.[4]

This paradigm, which structures and contextualizes experience, is produced by the imagination. For some, the world is a "jungle" that demands an aggressive posture in order to survive. For others, the technological age suggests a more logical, mechanical approach to life. Still others see life as most meaningfully portrayed in economic terms where people market their wares in an attempt to show a profit in terms of the maximization of pleasure and the minimization of pain.

Each of those paradigms suggests an operating image of reality. Each responds to certain questions, ignores others, and gives some idea of what is to be expected. Each carries a "promise" of sorts. According to Lynch, faith also constitutes a paradigm, a model, a way of inserting a person into reality. For Lynch, faith is most adequately seen as the Christic imagination characterized by its ironic qualities.[5]

---

4. William Lynch, "Faith, Experience and Imagination," *New Catholic World* 215, no. 1285 (July/August 1972): 170-71; *IF* 16-17.

Since faith is a certain type of imagination, it partakes of the qualities of the imagination. Faith makes images that put us in touch with reality. Borrowing from Lynch's definition of imagination, it might be said that faith constitutes "all the resources of man, all his faculties, his whole history, his whole life, and his whole heritage, all brought to bear upon the concrete world inside and outside of himself, to form images of the world, and thus to find it, cope with it, shape it, even to make it."[6] Thus, faith does not deal only with the "next world," or only part of this world. Just as there is a transcendental aspect to imagination, there is a transcendental aspect to faith, since it touches on all aspects of experience and reality.

The task of faith, then, is to imagine the real, and, as Lynch reminds us, "that [task] might also very well mean making the real, making the world, for every image formed by everybody is an active step, for good or for bad." The imagination never simply reproduces the reality it encounters. It also produces. The same may be said of faith. A simple "reproductive faith" would be as unrealistic as the concept of a simple "reproductive imagination." Under this approach, then, faith is not simply a mirror that reflects unseen realities; it is also a principle by which those realities are in part produced. Although Lynch did not use the term, we might speak of a "productive faith" that generates images that lead us to increasingly profound entrances to the real. As those images are encountered, adopted, lived, dramatized, prayed, expressed and reexpressed, a fuller participation in reality is gained. As the depths of the finite are tapped, the infinite divine begins to unfold its mysteries.[7]

An example of this "productive faith" may be found in the New Testament. It is common knowledge among scriptural exegetes that the Evangelists did not simply report the same facts. Of course, their stories are predominantly the same. There is a reproductive aspect to faith. But the Gospels do vary in significant ways. The differences are often attributed to the varying theologies

---

5. *IF* 14-15.

6. *CP* 23.

7. *CP* 23; id., "The Life of Faith and Imagination," 11; *IF* 64.

of the Evangelists. However, if faith is imagination, and if faith, therefore, may be seen as not only reproductive but productive, might we have four analogous faiths, not merely four analogous theologies? During the patristic age, the faith in the East developed differently from that in the West. Those in the East viewed sin in terms of sickness, and grace in terms of salvation. Those in the West viewed sin in terms of disobedience, and grace in terms of justification.[8] Since each faith is analogous to the other, it is true to say that they are the same. There is one faith. Yet it is also true to say that they are different. Communities as diverse as East and West can hold one faith as long as they can admit the analogous quality of faith that can, therefore, tolerate differences within the very heart of faith's identity. The faith of the Christian is not so simple that it can be contained in a single imagination or in a single imaginative framework. Perhaps it can be adequately expressed only in the actual life of the risen Jesus Christ.

The analogical character of faith suggests that each act of faith gives rise to a new, unique image of faith. Recall the example of the mouse that Lynch employed to explain the concept of analogy. This particular mouse has never existed before. Whatever image we may have had of a mouse previously, we will have to allow this particular mouse to show us something of what it means to be this particular rodent. Our image of what a mouse is capable of will be enriched accordingly.

Likewise with the images of faith. One might have a more or less sufficient image of a particular parish, say, in suburban middle America. If we move to a parish in the heart of the city, however, a very different image of what it means to be a parish will emerge – if we let it. The danger, of course, is that we may attempt to take one image of a parish and univocally apply it to analogous parish settings. When an image is imposed on a reality, the doctrine of emergence is violated, and our dealings with that reality are impoverished.

It follows, for instance, that a wealthy parish should produce images that call to mind its responsibilities of stewardship. Such a

---

8. See Stephen J. Duffy, *The Dynamics of Grace: Perspectives in Theological Anthropology* (Collegeville, Minn.: The Liturgical Press, 1993), 63-72.

parish might imagine itself as the "twin" of a poorer parish.[9] What it means for the richer parish to be a "twin" will differ substantially from what it means for the poorer twin. Poorer parishes should thrive on images that encourage people to value and develop their hidden powers and talents even in the midst of their weakness. For example, what it means for a wealthy parish "to carry the cross" will be quite different from what it means for the poor "to carry the cross." Again, the danger lies in the possibility that a person might view the image of "bearing the cross" in univocal terms so that the sacrifice of "giving till it hurts" might be expected of the poor in inappropriate ways that might lead to their further impoverishment. The poor must indeed carry the cross, but in terms of dying to their limited vision, dying to their resignation to "the way things are," in order to experience a life that is more fully human. Yet both rich and poor will indeed be carrying a cross.

In addition, believers must realize that their images are analogous to, not simply reproductive of, the real. That is, the images are both the same as and different from the reality they attempt to fathom. Furthermore, the "same" is situated right in the heart of the "different" because real entities themselves are analogues of being.[10]

Since true authentic faith is always analogical, faith does not attempt to separate opposites. The acknowledgment of the existence of pairs of contraries in life allows faith to remain humble. Hence, belief and unbelief reside together in the believer. People believe but they are not always quite sure whether they correctly understand the object of belief. If the act of belief is separated from unbelief, then a rigid, simplistic system emerges that will give believers difficulty grasping the more subtle dynamics of a revealing God. For example, if one should banish all taint of unbelief, then the results of the historical-critical biblical methods will generate more anxiety than faith. Lynch notes that those believers who dispel any inclination to unbelief

---

9. In such "twinning" relationships, the two parishes strike up a relationship to gain an appreciation of their cross-town brothers and sisters. The wealthier parish usually assumes some portion of the twin's debts until the twin can handle its own financial affairs.

10. *CA* 149.

. . . will believe only in the ideal and only mock the
present reality. Thus illusion and reality, faith and unfaith, will be neatly compartmentalized. . . . Anybody can
believe in the ideal; it is no great trick at all and takes
no effort . . . what is necessary is that we come with faith
and unfaith, with a sense of reality and illusion, belief
and criticism, high seriousness and mockery, to the same
reality in one and the same act.[11]

Lynch cautions that the Church should always recognize not only
the content but also the "hollowness" of its rhetoric. Ironically, its
faith may be constant only to the extent its "unfaith" is present.
Faith is always expressed in relative terms. That about which faith
speaks is absolute. That which it says is relative.[12]

Language embodies the imagination, and, hence, embodies
faith as well. When language functions well, the faith can be
vibrant. When a civilization suffers a breakdown in language,
when its words are no longer spoken credibly, when words begin
to mean their opposites, when objectivity is taken lightly, or when
the language devolves into slogans and catch words, then, Lynch
warns, language loses its relation to true faith, and only mimics
it, and, perhaps, may even mock it. Then language and its images
begin to distort reality rather than put us into relation to the real.[13]

B. Christic Irony

Christian faith is not merely the analogical imagination. It is the
ironic imagination that has engaged the life of Christ. Irony
educates faith because it de-absolutizes things. The ironic imagination accomplishes this by keeping relative opposites together in
a particular sort of way. In the ironic imagination, a thing comes

---

11. *IF* 93, 186. One is reminded of Newman's admonition that we can never
properly express the faith: "We can only set right one error of expression by
another. By this method of antagonism we steady our minds . . . by saying
and unsaying to a positive result." Unpublished *Theological Papers*, quoted in
John Coulson, *Religion and Imagination: "In Aid of a Grammar of Assent"*
(Oxford: Clarendon, 1981), 64.
12. Avery Dulles develops the same theme in chap. 9, "Doubt in the Modern
Church," in *Survival of Dogma* (N.Y.: Crossroad Publishing, 1971).
13. *IF* 68-69, *IH* 66.

through its opposite. Life comes through death, strength through weakness, exaltation through humility, and fullness through emptiness. Lynch sees irony as "a distinctive paradigm or patterning of facts, a re-composing in which a fact (e.g., 'having nothing') is seen within the creative presence of a contrary ('and possessing all things')."[14]

A certain "shock of irony" comes from the recognition that the unification of those contraries is not a mistake. But Christian irony does not consist in a mere juxtaposition of opposites. In Christian terms, lowliness is not only the instrument used to reach the high, it *is* the high. Lynch notes that the "*usual quality of irony is the unexpected coincidence, to the point of identity, of certain contraries.*" In Christian irony, there is more than merely a surprising coexistence of contraries. There is "an actual transformation of being." The adulteress can be transformed into a virgin with child in the same sense that the poor can be seen as wealthy.[15]

Christian faith proposes a certain type of ironic transformation. After all, there may be ironic transformations that work for evil rather than for good. For example, a good man's ordination taken in the wrong spirit may lead to a sort of clericalism that can constitute his downfall as well as the downfall of many others. Lynch specifies the ironic transformation of Christ:

> It involves the mastery of the world, spiritual freedom, freedom from the past and from every form of that which imprisons; it works through death and weakness; it therefore dethrones every other pretentious idea and establishes the movement through the human condition, and total human condition (not the human condition of the beautiful people) as the way. Weakness becomes one of the great forms of power. . . . Precisely what we are becomes the ironic mode of the transcendence of what we are.[16]

The Christic imagination is attained through an attentive appropriation of the paradigm of the life of Christ. The Christic

---

14. *IF* 102, 14.
15. *IF* 84-85, emphasis found in the original.
16. *IF* 101.

imagination attempts to maintain the pattern of transformation Christ effected throughout his life. The Christian believer does not hesitate to think divine thoughts, but he thinks them only as the same believer who also thinks very common thoughts. The promises of Christ reach us only through the death of Christ as it is experienced in the death of the believer. Otherwise, divine thoughts come rushing only too readily and transform people into mad dreamers. The human then is destroyed rather than redeemed.[17]

Lynch also noted that there has been a second creation. The risen Christ, though continuous with the particular historical Jesus, nevertheless begins to be included in a new imagination. Things become more radically themselves when seen in the light of Christ, more powerful, more filled with the energy of transformative possibilities. Thus, the cries of suffering children are transformed when they are heard within the cries of Christ. The cry of Christ increases the volume of the other cries and makes it impossible for us to ignore them. Christ has sublated the old order of imagination with a new imagination that "is a new level, identical in structure with, but higher in energy than, every form or possibility of the old." The new Christic imagination does not require us to place the image of Christ on everything we see. Just the opposite. Everything is seen in a new light – for what it really is in itself.[18]

Faith must befriend human frailty so that the divine presence can be felt. Productive faith thus must search for images that retain contraries such as strength and weakness on friendly and even ironic terms. Our Christic transformation is attained precisely in the embrace of who we are now: frail human beings created to perfect our freedom in love. The attainment of who we are as loving humans is the achievement of the gift of faith as productive of images that can shatter the limited confines of the comfortable worlds many of us tend to establish for ourselves, and can transform our vision to see the sacredness of even the lowliest of God's creatures, even as it did St. Francis's.

One cannot become presumptuous in living the faith. Presumption destroys the irony. It would turn a relationship of

---

17. *IF* 88.
18. *CA* 190, 192-93; *CP* 26, 39.

love into a mechanistic bargain more suited to the economic imagination. The lowly do not assume their positions in order to be exalted. They are lowly precisely because of their humility that is bereft of lofty aspirations. The language of faith, therefore, is not presumptuous, but it is open in hope. It follows that the language of faith is the humble language of irony, which always means more than it seems to say. Lynch observed,

> Rather than risk high language that does not carry the day faith will tend to use the language of understatement. The consequence will often be flat language and high meaning. Faith believes, but it is modest, so to speak, about itself and its own language.

But the language of faith is not merely strategically cautious. It does not speak in this way only because the infinite can be expressed only in finite terms. Lynch insists that irony is present only if its contraries enter into our feelings and judgments. He adds,

> That happens when faith is comic *and* serious, humble *and* firm, flexible *and* unequivocal, or when mockery turns out to be really serious. Irony and mockery often trap us, and then we discover that the argument was really serious.[19]

Faith is a paradigm that keeps the believer humble. It forms the world of the believer, but without the haughtiness of those who refuse to consider other paradigms as having some validity. Faith does not allow the believer to grasp the world. Faith allows the believer to be grasped by it, sometimes in surprising and unexpected ways.

C. The Light of Faith: A Peculiar Paradigm

As we have seen, faith generates a paradigm, a way of patterning the experiences and facts that come to us each day. Faith is the light in which we see the world. It is a paradigm of irony. Furthermore, Lynch maintained that faith is a "creative" or an

---

19. William Lynch, "Images of Faith II: The Task of Irony," *Continuum* 7 (1969): 481. Emphasis found in the original.

"active" paradigm that generates an active imagery. It does not simply carry forward the images of the past, but it reshapes or reforms those images according to those realities of the modern world that make the cross of Christ a cross that is redemptive of our own day, and not merely a relic of the past.[20]

Each age crucifies the Lord in a different way and therefore needs to be redeemed in a different way. A relevant image of redemption must be presented before redemption can be received in the depths of a person's life. The dramatists who persuade their audiences to "re-cognize" reality through their compelling use of images perform a valuable service for the faithful. When the ironic paradigm of faith meets the diffraction of good drama, new images of faith emerge and fresh profound meaning reemerges from those images that constitute the norms of our faith. Consequently, it may be said that the light of faith is a light that is ever new. It changes, grows, and constantly reveals profounder aspects of reality that had never quite struck home before.[21]

Lynch insists that faith be conceived also as a "moving paradigm," a paradigm that moves believers through every aspect of the finite in gaining their religious insight.[22] Faith moves into this world, not away from it. Faith allows a person's images to be flexible, to move with the requirements of reality. Faith frees people from their ruts. As believers appreciate the irony of the finite, they gain a taste of the infinite.

It should come as no surprise that faith as Christic imagination requires a body. As imagination, faith proposes that the world and its people ought to be approached in a certain way, in light of a definite set of sensibilities. Faith attempts to defeat indifference. Lynch claims that there is a "body of sensibility of faith" that helps to shape the imagination of believers, and that leads them on a journey through finite reality. In a sense, this light of faith has a body. Believers attempt to perceive God by the light of faith in Jesus. Thus, Jesus, in all his corporeality, can declare, "I am the light of the world."[23]

---

20. *IF* 14, 19.
21. *IF* 159; *CP* 23; *IF* 20-21, 23-24.
22. *IF* 23-24.

This body of sensibility of faith might be compared to Tradition. It constitutes a complex instrument that took thousands of years to develop. That instrument enables us to handle the experiences of life in such a way that they will strengthen and not destroy us. It is embodied in the "books, actions, histories, lives, . . . an atmosphere, and above all in the person of Christ. . . ." That sensibility, or the ability to respond with a passion appropriate to the area of experience encountered at a given moment, develops by virtue of the Holy Spirit's presence to this embodied experience of sensibility that the community has passed down through history. Thus, the light of faith is not simply the product of the present moment nor is it merely a personal affair. It is faith in Jesus Christ. It is the product of what has been given to us through centuries of Christian living: "You are the light of the world."[24]

Finally, in considering faith as the action of the dramatic imagination, Lynch packs that action with direction and meaning. Tradition not only teaches the faith from the inside, it constitutes action with a history and a goal, a past and a future. A healthy faith keeps moving in the present in view of the past, reaching toward the future. It does not become fixated on the past as if it were a time of ideal faith that needs to be recaptured for our own day, nor does it become so presumptuous of the future that it becomes comfortable with the cries of the poor in the present. Faith lives in promise. It lives in the hope of salvation.[25]

II. Faith as Salvation

Faith has long been recognized as a means of salvation, if not salvation itself (see Mk. 5:34; Lk. 7:50; Mt. 9:22; Jn. 14:12). As Lynch saw it, faith as imagination is a way of fitting into reality in such a fruitful way that it leads to our salvation.

---

23. *CP* 118; Jn. 8:12.
24. *IF* 63-64; id., "Faith, Experience and Imagination," 171; Mt. 5:14.
25. Id., "Faith, Experience and Imagination," 172-73.

A. Faith, Salvation, and Freedom

Every person seeks to "belong" to reality. No healthy person seeks isolated estrangement. Perhaps our primary wish is to be what God intends for us to be: human. Yet when we look for what we have, we find freedom among the most splendid of human faculties. There are at least two different ways freedom can be considered. It can be seen as an isolated autonomy in itself, and, therefore, in defiance of God, or it can be seen as an autonomy that is a grace of God, and, therefore, as salvation.[26]

Those who view human freedom as a competitor to God's freedom are victims of the "Promethean imagination." Lynch defines Prometheanism as a grandiose vision of the human as independent will and power. It recognizes no conditions on its freedom, whether those conditions come from inside or outside the human domain. Its expressions of freedom are exercises of sheer willfulness. The Promethean imagination urges a person to do something simply because it is possible, in response to some inner urge. As Prometheus stole fire and the arts from the gods, so this imagination is somewhat of a renegade. The Promethean person dares to think any thought and assault any sensibility – all in the name of freedom. Playing the role of a thief, such a person must suffer the consequences of theft: a nagging sense of guilt. If that type of autonomy is a theft, a defiance of reality, its freedom will not furnish a place in reality where the free person may be said to "belong." The discomfort of guilt will always follow.[27]

Redemption occurs when a person's autonomy can be viewed as a real autonomy yet also as a grace, not a defiance, of God. Autonomy is then exercised without guilt. Freedom then is established as the way God wants humans to be inserted in reality. Faith is the process of that insertion, and salvation is its result. The graced autonomy of a person emerges only from the condi-

---

26. *IH* 26-27; *CP* 7, 40. It is interesting that the Second Vatican Council uses precisely the term "autonomy" (*autonomia*) in promoting the idea that human autonomy comports with the will of God (*Gaudium et Spes*, Art. 36).

27. *CP* 64-65, 56ff., 17, 62. Lynch develops these thoughts in terms of the Promethean imagination when he deals with cultural issues, and in terms of the Dionysian imagination when dealing with individual personal issues. See *IF* 40-45.

tions of being human, and it operates within those conditions. Outside of those conditions, human autonomy is unconditioned by anything else. Thus, Lynch asserts that any human wish is justified merely because it is human. The human does not need to go outside of itself to seek permission to have such a wish.[28]

This claim is not as excessive as it might first appear. Lynch does not contend that a wish is justified merely because a person has it. For example, the Oedipal wish to kill one's father and marry one's mother is not expressive of human openness in love, but rather betrays a certain resistance to one's growth to maturity. It is a wish born of Promethean desires that acknowledge no boundaries. It is actually what Lynch prefers to describe as "willfulness." A person may not be guilty for having such a wish, but such wishes hardly qualify as "human." One is not autonomous in making such a wish – quite the opposite. One would seem to be enslaved to an urge born of pressures that are not completely evident. The "human" in such a case would call that person beyond himself to transcend such pressures through greater self-awareness, perhaps a healing of past woundedness, and through the performance of more mature acts of love in his present relationships.[29]

The wish, according to Lynch, is a positive, not a destructive, act of the imagination. It is for something, not against it. It is more the product of love than defiance. This human type of wish goes outside of itself, but not for permission to have the wish. That type of wish would be an alienated wish from the start. The human wish goes outside of itself in search of mutuality, not dominance or servitude.[30] As Lynch would say, my wish is valid simply because it is mine. The sole proviso is that it be a human wish. That is to say, the wish must be mine, not just partly mine, "partly" in the sense of its being really another person's wish, and also in the sense of its not being supportive of the whole of the "humanity" that I am. Mutuality assists a person in making human

28. Id., "The Task of Enlargement," 345; id., "Euripides' 'Bacchae,' " 164; *IH* 150, 172.
29. *IH* 144, 147. Rollo May, *Love and Will* (New York: Dell Publishing, 1969), 213-15.
30. *IH* 146, 171. Rollo May, *Love and Will*, 213-15.

wishes because that wish has now made contact with the outside world in a way that is creative of freedom. Mutuality signals that there is help, and thus, hope on the horizon.[31]

Faith therefore leads to a radical, premoral, human autonomy. This autonomy is "premoral" in the sense that it is that fundamental autonomy by which a person fashions a self that strikes a unique stance in this world. At this stage, the specific moral acts of a person are not as much at issue as the positing of an identity of the one who will choose to do this or that act. This is accomplished not only by the moral acts one performs but also by a host of other decisions, all of which contribute to one's identity. It is the freedom to be Hester, and not necessarily the Hester that fits a preestablished mold, Puritan or otherwise. In a sense, faith is a free assent to undertake anew the human project of autonomy which requires an imagination that can envision the autonomy within a creation in which it is not the sovereign. That is the task of faith as the analogical imagination: to see oneself and other people as autonomous yet dependent "others" of the "One" God of creation.[32]

One can see the doctrine of emergence in operation here. One ought not bring preconceived notions to dictate what is and what is not allowed to be human. The autonomy of the human will emerge with human life that is lived to the full, that is, in loving freedom and knowledge. Thus, a person ought to wish absolutely, but ought not turn the adverb "absolutely" into a noun by wishing for absolutes. If any created thing is given the status of an absolute, then freedom and autonomy have been forfeited, and an idol has been fashioned. Care must be shown even in calling God "absolute," since the tendency then would be to objectify God who is always subject.

B. Faith, Salvation, and Law

Of course, human autonomy is shaped by the human condition. The human includes conditions that are incumbent on our status

---

31. *IH* 169-71, 175-76.
32. *IH* 150, 172.

of being in relation to other people, animals, plants, and objects, as well as on our status of having a personal interior life. We have boundaries. That finitude is the first form of "law" that a person must obey.[33]

Our freedom is limited but, nevertheless, contains a wish to be all things, or to be without bounds. Given the right relations with others, all things are permitted. "Love and do what you will," as Augustine wisely counseled. But freedom comes ironically through the law. The goal is not freedom from the law, but freedom in it. It comes by passing through the narrow, finite, yet deep conditions of the human. This type of law is not superficial external law, but a law written on the inward heart. The principle of freedom in us embraces the principle of our finitude, or the "principle of Law," as Lynch calls it in this context. Through the interpenetration of those contraries, true freedom is attained. There is no logic that can explain it. Freedom's achievement becomes apparent not in theory, but only in action. Lynch offered the example of a poet who is freed to write more stirring poetry only when laws of a certain meter and rhyming scheme are obeyed. This is the Christic way, the way of the definite.[34]

Human freedom needs to be educated. The teacher who is experienced and adept at uniting, explaining, and rationally critiquing those experiences, who is open to further experiences, can guide the unexperienced. That is, human freedom is educated by allowing people the benefit of reliving vicariously the experiences of others and by illuminating those experiences through rational discussion so that the student may appropriate freely the insight of the teacher. That insight is not imposed from the outside. It is recreated on the inside as the student's own insight. Not only does the student retain freedom in this way, but each educational opportunity becomes an exercise of freedom. The teacher then can be seen as a source of liberty and creativity.[35]

Educated freedom comes from the sympathetic meeting of two insides, and the recognition of a common human spirit that

---

33. *IM* 63ff.; id., "The Problem of Freedom," 101-2.
34. Id., "The Problem of Freedom," 102-4, 113; *IH* 151; *IM* 72, 75.
35. Id., "The Problem of Freedom," 104-5, 108.

yearns genuinely to discover and to create the human condition. Salvation is the satisfaction of that yearning without guilt. It is attained through faith which, as imagination, provides the ability to see the unseen, as well as the ability to nurture the human interiority that is the grace of God. Graced action then becomes possible. Faith touches the inside of people through the images it employs, and it wins their freedom, their position in reality, through the law:

> Under grace a man does not obey the Law out of a spirit
> of necessity which would make all law doubly Law, but
> out of an inward groaning and desire of the Holy Ghost
> for very love of reality. For all reality, but especially for
> homely, concrete reality, the world of the real God of
> Abraham, Isaac, and Jacob.

The law now becomes "both the free act of man and an act of God himself, of that Holy Spirit who operates in us."[36]

The image of Christ, which faith nurtures, should bring us to that point of autonomy under God. The faithful person adopts Christ as the law: to do what Christ did or would have done out of love for him. Unless that Christic choice is made and confirmed in action, freedom remains only a theoretical possibility. At that point, the law vanishes as law. It is love. It commits itself in action freely taken. Certainly banished is any conception of law that fixes everything for the faithful. If the law could speak, Lynch claims that it would say,

> I cannot and will not do for you what mothers are
> expected to do for those who are still children, namely,
> determine the future and explain every possible variation
> of myself which you will meet. In a word, I determine
> everything and I determine nothing.

That is why it is necessary for faith to contain and to create constantly the impossible image of Christ every day. It is "impossible" because no mere image can contain Christic life, but it is "necessary" because the closest one can come to another person is through images. At that ultimate point of law called love as it is

---

36. Ibid., 113, 114.

expressed in the person of the Son of God, "we embrace in the one act the finite humanity of Christ and the Infinite God, the limit and the unlimited, law and freedom."[37]

A faith that commits itself to the life of Christ, therefore, must see the image of Christ as that which continues the expansive way of life shown by Jesus. Christ is the opener of life, the liberator, the one who enlarges life, not the theoretical model that is turned into an ideology to foreclose the possibilities of human development. The memory of Christ that is held in the images of faith should give the believer a past that can be productively united with a Christian set of images for the future that give the present a redemptive direction. The image of Christ is redemptive because through it we come in contact with one who lived and died a truly free life in the past, but is now risen and alive, and is eschatologically situated in glory with the Father.[38]

C. Faith, Salvation, and the Will of God

It follows that the will of God is not simply found in external laws, but in the redemptive direction that is possible in any life. It is found precisely in the ability of people to formulate free human wishes that have truly emerged from their own hearts. God has not mapped out the course of each human life, establishing one particular "right way" that each individual must travel "or else" face the consequences of displeasing God. As people move from an old hypothesis through the passage of suffering to a new hypothesis, they do so as free, intelligent agents using the gifts and experiencing the limitations present within their lives.[39]

Nevertheless, faith does direct the course of a life to the extent that it can control the infinite possibility of a rampant Promethianism that has no respect for human boundaries. Lynch claimed that promise and Providence give direction to the many possible wishes people may formulate. Promise and Providence coalesce in the subjective decisions and commitments that are

---

37. *IM* 95, 72, 75, 96; id., "The Life of Faith and Imagination," 11.
38. *CP* 70, 72; *IH* 213.
39. *CP* 94-95; id., "Toward a Theology of the Secular," 361-62; *IH* 143, 173-74.

made in light of God's promises to the human race as they have been revealed through Noah, Abraham, Moses, and Jesus. In a sense, faith itself keeps infinite possibility under control through the internalization of those promises as they are found in the covenants. They establish an orientation. "For one thing, since faith and the love of God have no taste for evil they will have no commerce with it, will instinctively avoid it." As the future unfolds, promise directs infinite possibility through its power to set limits. "I decide to elaborate my identity not only into the past but into the future as well." God's Providence also constitutes a binding of infinite possibility, but not quite as we limit it through our vows, promises, and plans. God's promise is that of unlimited hope. There can be a better or a worse future, and, therefore, a better or a worse hope, but there will never be a future without hope. God binds infinite possibility through the unexpected, the ironic structure of the divine presence.[40]

God's will is simply that we experience the redemptive power of love. How is that to be accomplished? God may well be imagined as responding, "You decide!" That is why people were graced with an autonomy that can love and a mind that can think. Otherwise love would not really be love. So our task is to be human and to show God what it means to be human from one's own vantage point. We have a model of one who has done precisely that with his life: Jesus Christ.

The person's response to God comes in a way that is unique, though not solipsistic. Hester Prynne does not need to show God, indeed, cannot show God, what it means to be human. But she can show God something of what it means to be Hester Prynne, and in that concrete way express something of what humanity means. Salvation is not a desperate attempt to be something other than what we are, nor is it the abdication of our God-given responsibility to be free. Guilt is not confined to acts of Promethean willfulness that ignore human boundaries. Guilt can also arise if a person attempts to limit the human to only a portion of what it is or could be. It is the person who is not fully alive, but is only partially alive. It is the person who gives up the

---

40. *IF* 154-55.

burden of responsibility. The guilty prefer not to think, not to struggle, not to endure the pathos that comes with the search for the ever new light of faith. Some suppress the intellect, attempting to respond to God only through what they feel God is "telling" them to do. Others suppress the feelings, believing that a logical plan for life has been laid out before them. Neither group fully accepts the responsibility of freedom, and neither group fully realizes the power of love in their lives.[41]

Those who live such partial lives would do well to seek a deeper faith through a conversion of the operative images in their lives. Such a movement, of course, requires courage and ability to let go that is expected of the way leading from *drama* through *pathos* to *mathos*. It requires an extraordinary effort, yet it is an effort that takes place to a greater or lesser extent in every human life. Lynch claims that we constantly form and reform the world and its countless images that come to us each day. We conquer the world of chaos through the imagination, always seeking to dispel the endlessness or senselessness in what we encounter. As more adequate images of the human are adopted (as the life of Christ is taken more seriously), a more adequate new light of faith begins to dawn.[42]

Lynch claims that the qualities of *mathos*, or the new light, or, as applied to this context, the light of faith, reveal that what had been a trap in the old hypothesis has sprung open in freedom.[43] A new unconditionality is perceived, and therefore a new possibility for self-possession, self-expression, and love. Furthermore, a shift from a cosmocentric to an anthropocentric image of the world is implied. In other words, our particular way to the human will not be seen as something that is written somewhere outside the human heart. The endless search outside

---

41. *CP* 70.

42. Id., "Introduction: On the Transformation of Our Images," *New York Images: A Journal of Places, Arts, Literature*, no. 3 (Autumn 1986): 3; *CP* 77.

43. The "trap" describes an old solution that no longer works in present circumstances, and, in fact, even begins to aggravate the problem. The more it is pursued, the tighter the trap closes. The trap can be constituted by practically any of our operating conceptions – those of justice, equality, freedom, goodness, or even faith itself. Faith as a trap will be treated in the concluding chapter. The light of faith as *mathos* illuminates a way out of the trap.

the self for "the rules" can come to an end with the discovery of our own sense of what it means to be human from the inside. We are already human, and we need not trust an abstraction.[44]

This new dawning of the light of faith as *mathos* also implies a movement from a mechanistic moral system that concentrates on outward actions toward an ethical stance that focuses on the human autonomy of the person. It pays attention to the quality of love that a person brings to expression. As inward illumination is seen as the grace of God, the secular project of letting things emerge on their own terms becomes a truly human, and therefore a sacred project. Reverence then becomes an important ethical dimension of every human decision. Ironically, a search for innocence must also be undertaken to conquer the inevitable feelings of guilt that arise when anything radically new makes its appearance on the human scene.[45]

D. Faith, Salvation, and Admiration

Insofar as faith furnishes us with an analogical imagination, there is hope for salvation because it is then possible to make actual contact with reality. Contact with reality is important because that is where God is found. Lynch proposed that admiration is an important tool of salvation that enables people to contact reality because it constitutes a movement "from the self, out of the self, into reality."[46]

Here Lynch clearly perceived the many forms of the modern movement into the self. To the extent that a person remains imprisoned in the self, a certain madness takes hold. Lynch noted that shame seduces people to withdraw to their inner selves. The pain of ridicule, the discomfort of knowing that one is a laughingstock, slams the prison door shut.

---

44. *CP* 94-95, 97.

45. *CP* 35, 101ff.

46. William F. Lynch, "A Book of Admiration: A Prose Poem on the Forms of Salvation," unpublished manuscript at the Fordham University archives (undated), 1. Hereinafter cited as "*BA*." Lynch was still working on this remarkable book at the time of his death.

What is needed for release from this form of damnation? Contact with reality, not with ideals, but with the real world that one can touch, feel, hear, see, smell, and taste. Lynch urged us to consider the example of Ajax, who was, next to Achilles, the greatest Greek warrior known to the ancients. This noble soldier was not only denied the honor of receiving the armor of the fallen Achilles, but worse still, he was deceived by the goddess Athena into believing that a herd of pigs was actually the group of Greek leaders that he had determined to kill in revenge. Madly, he attacked them, only to be awakened to the stupidity and the shame of what he had done. The culture, Lynch notes, made it impossible for Ajax to master his shame. The culture was based on honor and fame. There was no place for a shamed individual to show his face. Lynch sympathized with Ajax, "How great a fool can you make of a man before you drive him so far inward that it is impossible for him to admire or love anything." The "shaming imagination" perverts reality to the point where the shamed individual cannot see those who could perhaps help him the most. In the case of Ajax, salvation was extended to him through his mistress-wife, his infant son, and his brother, Teucer. Ultimately Ajax falls on the great sword of Hector, thus ending his agony, but not his shame. Such is a story of damnation.[47]

Could his story have been otherwise? Yes. The ironic Christic imagination makes it possible to admire the fool. Lynch notes that Ajax's loving wife, Tecmessa, did not need reasons to admire him. Nor did his infant son need to be convinced of the honor of Ajax. Their bondedness to him remained intact. If only Ajax could have imagined his world enough to make some contact with it, he would have experienced salvation, and not the damnation of his self-imposed inward journey. Ajax was destroyed by the ideal. He opted not for his wife and son, but for an "empty interior where one gets a grip on nothing."[48]

One ought not fear the ugly. It is part of the real world. Ajax could not be saved by the beautiful, the neat, as if he could make a clean break from his past. It is an ugly experience to suffer

---

47. *BA* 14, 15.
48. *BA* 20-21.

the laughter of those who could otherwise supply honor and reverence. But the only way to reenter the real world was to hear the laughter it would entail.

Ajax would have to exchange the nothingness of despair for the nothingness that is the prelude to creativity. This nothingness requires a "struggle with strangeness, newness, possibility." Humiliation is a dirty affair by definition. It is ugly. But it also allows one reentrance to the real world. It allows one to see again, and to admire the really beautiful along with the ugly. What would a saved Ajax look like? Lynch offered an alternative ending:

> He has walked back, perhaps not without struggle, into the world, where the imagination works on its only possible material in the world, the human, and does not seek victory but unity with the world. . . . A star has appeared among us and salvation has come among us. The Lord in unimagined form. The crowds are gathering. The word is growing. Somebody lights a candle and then another. The joke, a good one, spreads round the city. . . . But how natural. . . .[49]

The walk back into the City of Man creates apprehensions. This time the walk will be new and fearful. But the perturbation does not destroy, it rather signals possibility. It is a sort of "fear of the Lord." It signals the beginning of the risk of a venture. This troubling descent into the self produces an ascent, a "prelude to the making of the admirable."[50]

There are many ways in which people can reestablish contact with reality. There are many paths to salvation, many human materials that can assist us on the way back. "It all began with Prometheus," Lynch mused,

> who descended alone from among the gods to lead men through the beginnings of the jungle of possibility by teaching men the alphabet. Consider, as a grain of sand, what has come out of the alphabet and how we would have trembled if we really had known what was to come of all that. I admire the letter *A*, or its equivalent, as first

49. *BA* 39, 49, 46-47.
50. *BA* 49.

literary quantum because of what came out of it, all over the world.[51]

Lynch was not the only one who could appreciate how much could come from the letter A. Hester Prynne's skillful needlework in crafting the letter A attracted the attention and the admiration of those she encountered. Her artistry became an avenue to herself and to others. As that symbol became transformed from a badge of shame to an emblem of "Atonement" worn by an "Angel" regarded with "Affection," she and her neighbors began to make contact with each other, and, therefore, with reality. Hester was saved because she could rediscover herself and her God through a creative encounter with others, as well as expand her spiritual horizons through discovering newer and deeper possibilities of love. Thus did Hester defeat shame, a feat that neither Ichabod Crane nor even the mighty Ajax could achieve.

The work of the imagination is thus critical in its ability to produce images that allow a person to contact reality successfully. Lynch considered the Christic ironic imagination as an instrument of salvation precisely because of its power to lead us out of our private little hells that can seem so comforting at times. Thus, ". . . imagination *itself* is the great salvific enemy of narcissism, solipsism, [and] reductionism." Furthermore, Lynch noted that in salvation there is a certain transformation of images in which self and others are seen in a new light.[52]

To the extent that we reach out with a ironic Christic imagination in an effort to see each other in a new light, we bring the light of faith to bear on our world so we can see it, touch it, contact it, and experience salvation through the reality that the grace of God offers to us each day.

---

51. *BA* 50.
52. Id., "Imagining Past, Present, Future," 69; *BA* 34.

III. Faith and Reason

A. Faith and Knowledge

The relationship between faith and reason is perhaps most clearly seen when Lynch considers faith as a paradigm for gathering and fitting together the many pieces of information that come to us each day. In a sense, the question of whether knowledge or faith comes first in a believer's life is a false question. Both fideists and rationalists are wrong. There is no paradigm without a set of facts to assemble, and, conversely, there are no facts without a paradigm according to which they may be gathered in some intelligible way. Faith is a way of experiencing, not a separate additional experience. There is no faith without knowledge, and there is no knowledge without faith.[53]

Lynch claims that faith precedes what people ordinarily call knowledge. There is an initial faith, not necessarily an accurate faith, that all people have from birth. It is a raw faith, or a minimally formed way of receiving the experiences we have. Without faith "the mind cannot enter into existence at all, even at the most elementary point." It is this "primal faith" that does not necessarily have a religious sense. Lynch defines it as

> a primal and broad force of belief, promise and fidelity which, – by its presence or absence, by its operation or collapse, by its goodness or fury, by its fidelities or treacheries – shapes (or misshapes) the welfare, shall I say the very existence, of men and women in life and society. This force, and all the powerful experiential elements that belong to it should be imagined as moving historically into and up to a religious context, especially under the educating action of the promises of God and the reactions of men; but the movement is such that all this broad and primal life remains integral to religious faith as its body.[54]

Such primal faith is present from birth. Reality thus begins to be received after a fashion. Where it is absent, "experience" as such

---

53. Id., "Faith, Experience and Imagination," 170.
54. *IF* 37, 11, 9, 10; *IM* 10.

cannot be said to take place. A maddening fury fills the vacuum when the paradigm of a primal faith cannot handle certain events. The force of primal faith shapes the very existence of the child, and its anticipation of a future. Indeed the very womb of the mother, Lynch claims, constitutes a promise to the infant.

If Erik Erikson is correct, the issue of trust becomes the first central emotional concern of the child. That issue of trust or faith begins to fashion the child's horizontal or person-to-person relationships. It is a faith that has some facts, but lacks, one might say, experience in experiencing. It is unaware of the many ways facts may be assembled. Primal faith constitutes an "enormous primitive force in man that is not yet educated," but is just beginning to feel its relation to the world. Primal faith participates in a person's struggle to exist in this world. It can be enraptured by the beauty it perceives. It is "mad and visionary," and it has not yet appreciated the ironic dimension of life. Primal faith needs to be educated.[55]

When knowledge comes, it comes to educate faith. This education begins with the mother's first caresses of her infant. We might say that this is part of "the body of faith" that the child will encounter as it grows within a community of faith. Infant baptism forms another element of this embodied faith. It is a sign of the direction in which this primal faith is to grow: it is to grow in the body of sensibility in which the Holy Spirit has been active during the Christian millennia. The child of faith is to be brought up to receive certain experiences in certain ways. The world is not only a "jungle," giving evidence of original sin but is also a "garden" in which God's kingdom may break forth through our instrumentality.[56]

Faith necessarily has such a body. Otherwise it would hardly touch the human. It would languish at the level of an ideology that barely has anything at all to do with life. If faith is embodied, it needs pictures, stories, images, symbols, sacraments, Scripture, dogma, songs, leadership, sentiments, history, statues, rosaries, catechisms, coffee socials after Mass, devotions of vari-

---

55. *IM* 10; *IF* 60, 40-42.
56. *IF* 63.

ous kinds, even committee meetings that inevitably mix business with pleasure. They do not compromise the whole of faith, but they all belong. Throughout a lifetime, faith is educated by these embodied forms. They become a source of knowledge for faith. Thus, Lynch sees faith not only as an originating center but also as a result, a conclusion, a "developed construct of character, sensibility, judgments, images, reaction."[57]

All those elements participate in the shaping of a person's life. Of course, if any one element begins to occupy a disproportionate place in the life of the believer, both his life and the faith will suffer for it. Some elements are more important than others. Dogma, for example, constitutes an acknowledgment that faith as imagination contains an extraordinary mixture of predecision and freedom. As a people become members of the Catholic faith community, they begin an exploration into the real, but it is an exploration that has already chosen one orientation rather than another. It has rejected the Pelagian impossibility of excluding God's grace from human salvation, and it has excluded the Manichaean rigidity of separating spiritual from material reality. Even though many times those battles need to be fought again and need to be won on the personal level, they are struggles that the Church has already determined as a community. The Church offers her history of dogma as a guiding light for we try to appropriate those dogmatic victories in ways that are meaningful to the experiences of our own day.[58]

The instruments of faith, of course, may be misused. The devil himself may quote Scripture. Some people misuse dogma through their attempts to transform dogma into ideology. Dogma, properly understood, always contains a greater degree of unknowing than knowing. Its pronouncements, usually negative judgments, are analogical. Its roots spring from a specific concrete history, which is to say that its roots are real and contain all the limitations of the real. God is not found in dogma; rather dogma moves us toward authentic freedom and reality where God *is* found. These dogmas may be misused by those who call for

---

57. *IF* 64.
58. Id., "Theology and the Imagination," 65.

devotion, not to the God to whom the dogma points, but to the dogma itself. Sheer loyalty makes for a poor imitation of faith. Dogmatism thus can become a sort of idolatry that elicits commitment to a fixed form that results in a sort of slavery to a world of theory and abstraction. Extreme clarity can be just as harmful as extreme confusion because both extremes give up the analogical quality of true statements.[59]

Lynch was aware that his use of the term "faith" differed from the way Scholastics used it. He did not reject their theology, but, rather, he saw that Scholastics responded to a specific historical faith crisis by using perhaps the best tools then available to the Church. Their theology attempted to respond to a crisis which promoted the total rejection of the supernatural dimension in the cultural, intellectual and political sphere of their day. In fighting reductionist attacks, Church leaders attempted to respond pastorally so that common clerics would be able to communicate the faith to their parishioners in a way that would display the supernatural dimension clearly and simply. The foremost need was not academic achievement, but the pastoral care of the faithful. Lynch explained,

> Historically it had become crucially important to maintain a world and a vocabulary in which the supernatural is absolutely superior to every form of human knowledge and experience. This will always be crucial and necessary. But in the meantime other needs have risen for the solution of which this vocabulary has no special talent.[60]

It was in hopes of responding to modern needs that Lynch proposed his new vocabulary, employing its grammar of irony.

B. The Evidence of Things Unseen

Because faith reaches out into the mystery of the unseen God, it has become concerned with evidence. While faith cannot be reduced to the rational, nevertheless, the faithful seek affirmation that the act of faith is rational.

---

59. Ibid., 553 n. 25; *IH* 81-82.
60. Id., "Faith, Experience and Imagination," 170.

Lynch would agree that faith needs evidence, but *"it is found, collected and composed by faith itself."* Faith is a creative, not merely a reproductive, force within us. Yet faith is not sight. It is always reaching for the new hypothesis, always mixed with *pathos*, until the final days. Lynch claims that our faith transforms facts into evidence. First, we experience a relationship of trust. Then we find, even make, the evidence that supports that relationship of trust. The very act of amassing the evidence is motivated and governed by an overarching hypothesis of faith. Seemingly contrary evidence is no longer seen as contrary, but as supportive of faith. "Just as the good man finds the good, so faith finds evidence." Faith cannot be proven by the evidence; it can only be considered and then be accepted or rejected by the way we live our lives. We take a risk in adopting the point of view of faith, yet even if we reject a certain faith, that too is a risk because we must have some sort of faith as an operating view of reality, even if by default.[61]

In a sense, faith as imagination itself becomes a "shaping originator," a source, of knowledge. Given the power of images to think, faith is a way of progressing in knowledge. Reality approached with love yields secrets that are kept from the cynical. Yet Lynch insists that there are facts that no degree of faith will ever attain, such as the experience of death. Some things we simply do not know.[62]

---

61. *IF* 53, 126; *IH* 123-34. Emphasis found in the original. One is reminded of Newman's tapestry that is finally viewed on its correct side. There are no additional threads, but they are seen differently. We might also recall Rousselot's theory of reciprocal causality where the hypothesis and its supporting evidence necessarily come in one act. There is no story without the evidence, and there is no evidence without the story.

62. Although Lynch avoids a crass propositional approach to faith, he does acknowledge that in a sense faith does add something to our knowledge. Although the question of what Christ contributes to knowledge is good, Lynch considers it less productive than the question of what it contributes to the "guidance and ultimate destiny of faith." Put in those terms, the question yields two answers: (1) that reality contains a promise in the Easter mystery; and (2) that the promise involves the Christic irony of the Incarnation. Id., "Images of Faith II," 491; id., "Death as Nothingness," 459.

C. Faith and Rationality

The relationship between faith as imagination and rationality is usually approached as if faith's images could be placed alongside "rationality" to see whether those images "measure up." In that way, some theologians would hope to assess whether an image is reasonable. Theologians have also proposed to critique faith's imagination by placing it alongside cultural norms to see whether the image is believable for a particular culture. They also might take an image of faith and match it up against the tradition to see whether it is faithful to the Christian tradition as we understand it today. Such approaches are understandable in light of the recognition that the imagination needs certain restraints. It cannot be allowed to run rampant on its own.

But those strategies do not enter into the approach of William Lynch. Rationality, culture, and tradition are not separated from images so that images can be placed alongside "rationality," for example. A certain rationality, culture, and tradition are carried right within the image itself. Lynch would add that the image also carries something of human experience, decisions of the will, and a certain sensibility. Thus, the rationality, culture, tradition, experiences, choices, and sensibilities of one image can be called upon to critique the rationality, culture, tradition, experiences, choices, and sensibilities of another image. When we refer to "rationality" in a formal logical sense, it is really an abstraction from the operation of a selected group of images that illustrate a limited range of external relationships.[63]

But might there be a type of rationality other than formal logic, a type illustrated by the operation of other images that are more adept at showing certain internal relationships to us? The danger is that we might assume logic to be the only "rationality," and we might begin to impose that conception on all forms of

---

63. Even when dealing with external physical relationships, rationality still depends on the images that are employed. Consider the conflicting rationalities that are evidenced in the general theory of relativity, Newtonian physics, and quantum mechanics. See Stephen Hawking, *A Brief History of Time: From the Big Bang to Black Holes* (New York: Bantam Books, 1988), 19-20, 28-29, 65-67. Strictly speaking, an irrational image would not be an image at all – such as a "square circle."

reality. We might thereby unwittingly disregard the other types of rationalities that have a profound claim on us. The more usual univocal approach to rationality is understandable, but uncritical. It usually fails to acknowledge to which brand of images its "rationality" is beholden.

Lynch's point may be illustrated through a consideration of various scriptural images. For example, there are plenty of images of the compassionate Jesus in Scripture. These have rightfully enjoyed a certain pride of place in Christian theology. They present us with a certain "rationality" of compassion. The lost are pursued and saved, not simply forgotten. Compassion goes so far that it many times is precisely culturally incredible. Jesus' actions or parables often, therefore, constitute a critique of the culture. For example, Jesus, assuming a very anticultural stance, speaks with the woman at the well in a way that is intended to heal her and give her the spiritual resources to elevate the dignity in her life. That image was culturally very hard to swallow in Jesus' day, as was the image of a "Good Samaritan."

Consider the image of Paul instructing Onesimus, the slave, to return to his master, Philemon. Paul appeals to a certain Christian rationality that should enable Philemon to see Onesimus as a brother. Of course, we do not know whether Onesimus returned, but we might judge the image to be short on "human experience." It would be nice in a perfect world if Philemon were to receive Onesimus back and set him free. But one could also imagine a certain hesitancy on the part of Onesimus to test the faith of Philemon. The image is a challenging one that carries a certain rationality of its own, but it is culturally weak and experientially tenuous. It does speak of a certain sensibility that Christians ought to have with respect to one another, and it does carry the tradition. Finally, it commits one to a decision of the will that is not always easily made.

How might we treat the images of the crucified Jesus as risen and mingling with his disciples? Christians many times glibly accept the Resurrection with hardly a second thought. But what is so "rational" about the Resurrection? It is certainly outside of normal human experience, and certainly not expected culturally or even traditionally at the time of Jesus (even the Pharisees did not expect a resurrection until the end of time). The image of the Resurrection carries its own rationality, and it becomes a critique of other rationalities. It also establishes a tradition and critiques the culture. Now death can be treated with a whole new sensibility that mourns but also hopes. One's will to take up the cross acquires a whole new dimension that sees life through death as the way of love, the way of Jesus.

But the image of the Resurrection can be misunderstood. One might view it not as a giving or surrendering of one's life, but as an exchange. "I know why Christ mounted the cross!" this enthusiast exclaims. "It is because he was convinced that the glory he would receive after his death would be so much better than what he had in this world. I would march to the cross too if I were so convinced of my heavenly reward!" This statement is more suited to the economic imagination than to the Christic ironic imagination. The image of the crucified Christ crying out, "My God, my God, why have you forsaken me?" presents us with a view from the cross that ought to jar those who plan to bargain at the moment of death. It constitutes a critique of the economic imagination's distortion of the meaning of the Resurrection. Jesus' cry from the cross speaks of a sensibility that is in one way baffling, but, on the other hand, completely understandable from the viewpoint of human experience.

Now take another, less popular, image of Jesus. Jesus confronts the leaders of the Jews and says, "Were God your father, you would love me. . . . [But] the father you spring from is the devil" (Jn. 8:44). Immediately, exegetes and theologians alike scurry about for explanations. Why? This image of Jesus does not "fit" with the others. It is lacking in sensibility, its rationality is vindictive and biting, it is willful in the worst sense, and it is certainly contrary to the culture and tradition of Jesus' day. One would surmise that it is probably a vestige of the early Church's feuding with the Jewish establishment. Nevertheless, there it is.

How is it that we so immediately and instinctively eliminate such an image from our picture of Jesus, or allow it into our gallery of images only on the most qualified of terms? Lynch would contend that it is because of our faith, which experiences images together in a certain way. The images of Jesus taken together form a paradigm. That paradigm is called faith. Those images may be assembled in many different ways – ways that are compatible with the economic imagination, a prejudiced imagination, or a Christic ironic imagination, to name just a few. One imagination will give a favored status to Jesus' cry on the cross, while another will focus on the glorious and the miraculous, while yet another will give prominence to that which tends to separate Christians from Jews. Not all ways of assembling these images are equally faithful to Jesus. The devil himself can quote Scripture and can assemble its images according to taste. The difference is in the totality of images and in what they embody. The totality, the whole taken in a certain sort of way (a faithful way), tells us which images of faith are favored and in what context they are most meaningfully employed.

Thus, Lynch asserts that thought is mainly a struggle for right images. Images think. Each image presents a rationality. One may be tempted to overstate the case by claiming that there are as many different rationalities as there are different images and ways of putting those images together. Perhaps it would be better to say that there are as many rationalities as there are "root metaphors."[64] The same with cultures, traditions, experiences, sensibilities, and choices.[65] It is rather like the stitched "Jesus"

---

64. Paul Ricoeur describes root metaphors as follows: "One metaphor, in effect, calls for another and each one stays alive by conserving its power to evoke the whole network. Thus within the Hebraic tradition God is called King, Father, Husband, Lord, Shepherd, ... The network engenders what we call root metaphors, metaphors which, on the one hand have the power to bring together the partial metaphors borrowed from the diverse fields of our experience and thereby to assure them a kind of equilibrium. On the other hand, they have the ability to engender a conceptual diversity, I mean, an unlimited number of potential interpretations at a conceptual level. Root metaphors assemble and scatter." Paul Ricoeur, *Interpretation Theory: Discourse and the Surplus of Meaning* (Fort Worth: Texas Christian University Press, 1976), 64. As such, it seems that root metaphors carry a rationality so profound that they cannot be simply translated into concepts. See also Michael Cook, "Salvation as Metaphoric Process," *Theological Studies* 47, no. 3 (September 1986): 389 n. 4.

65. They are all beholden to images that together critique themselves in terms of the way they are grouped together. That is why faith is important for those who aspire to engage in theology. Those without faith tend to give undue prominence to images that the faithful consider secondary or even beside the

signs that have been quite widely circulated during the past decade or so. By cleverly blending the letters with the border, one might see the word "Jesus" immediately, but one might just as well see only a nondescript background that forms no word at all. Let each stitch in the needlepoint stand for a Scriptural image of Jesus. Nothing can force a person to assemble those images in one way rather than another. Yet some look at those stitches and see "Jesus," while others look on the very same stitches and see only a baffling incoherence. Faith is the way we put those images together. It is given by the whole. Individual images are interpreted in light of the whole, that is, in light of the grace of faith, or in light of the analogy of faith.

It is rather like John Henry Newman's example of the tapestry that is finally viewed on its artful side. There are the same threads, the same images (or image-stitches in our example) that come into play, but in a much different way. The way those images, those experiences of Jesus, are collected is faith. Thus, faith bears an intrinsic, not an extrinsic, relationship to reason, culture, tradition, experience, sensibility, and choice. It is a paradigm that is open-ended. It is incomplete. One of its messages is to tell of its very own incompleteness and to remind us that however loving we may consider ourselves to be, there is still a need for a Parousia. In some profound senses the Kingdom is here, but it is also true that it is not yet.

IV. Faith and Time

Because faith is not confined to a univocal conception of "the rational," it maintains a profound relationship with time. If faith were rational only in the sense of formal logic, time could simply be left behind in favor of timeless theories that have no need of a history. Indeed, some have valued an effort to escape from time as a desirable aid to faith.[66]

---

point. Those without faith do not offer a theology, but a critique of faith. Sometimes they raise good points. Various critiques and their hermeneutics of suspicion are important. But other times they critique a faith that is not held by the faithful.

A. Faith and the Acceptance of Time

Consistent with his insights concerning the finite, Lynch considers time as an essential dimension of faith. The experience of time should be intensified, not eliminated, in our search for the sacred. After all, time makes growth, promise, fulfillment, and redemption possible. There can be no salvation history without time. Hence Lynch claims that time does not need to be redeemed, rather it is the vehicle of redemption. It needs to be explored fully as Christ explored it, so that as time expires for a faithful person, that person's exploration may be crowned with resurrection and not disintegration. The "end of time" in the Christian sense should not be taken to mean that the time dimension has somehow been abstracted out of our lives. At the "end of time," the Christian hopes to experience time on an analogous level as the fullness of growth rather than the triumph of decay.[67]

Time might be described in terms of a sort of dying and rising. We must die every moment to the present as a new present continually rises before us. That which dies is the same as that which rises. "The temporal flow of human life is therefore a *formed* thing, a significant form." By this movement through the finite, one moment dying and giving rise to the next, a person moves into the infinite. Through time, we penetrate the finite in a sequential, and even consequential, way. This series of finite experiences and insights through the process of death and rising constitutes time itself.[68]

Enclosed within the very structure of time is the redemptive Paschal mystery. As we submit to the time process, it becomes apparent that time is not the enemy, but the way out of the trap. Time does not eliminate the past as if our sins never existed. It includes the past in the present dying-and-rising moment in hopes of the "nevertheless" of an irony that can include such a past in a redemptive moment yet to come.[69]

---

66. *CA* 38.
67. *CA* 51; *CP* 136.
68. *CA* 38-39.
69. *CA* 40-41.

Of course, time can be experienced in different ways. It can come as the endless, boring repetition of a machine. A change occurs as the dial advances across the face of a clock, and, therefore, time has passed. But it is not "human" time. Humans keep time to the beat of a Strauss waltz. There are high points and low points. There are moments of opportunity and moments of repetition. There are moments filled with sound and moments of syncopated silence that ironically seem to store up the entire momentum of the sound of music. Human time is the grace of opportunity to show once more the power of the inside, the sacred, to transform its finite outside. Human time is open, and it leaves room for the operation of the ironic. "Neurotic time" is suffered by a human trying to live completely within the confines of machine time. It is closed, and it leaves no room for anything that cannot be calculated. As Christians live their lives of faith, they move through time with the memory of a Tradition moving with them. It waltzes them through the present in a particular sort of way, suggesting new possibilities in hopeful anticipation of the notes to come.[70]

Lynch recommends that Christians trust the present as they move through time. Those who view the present as being valuable only in light of the future tend to turn the Resurrection into an image of desperation. Hope does not simply come from the future. The present contributes decisively to our hope in the way it produces energy to maintain the promise, as well as in its role in creating the future. Memory of the past also supports our hope in the promises through such events as the life, death, and resurrection of Jesus Christ.[71]

B. Stages of Life and Faith

As an illustration of the relationship between time and faith, Lynch proposed seven stages that might occur in the life of one who

---

70. *CA* 45; *IF* 109. Lynch described the two levels in terms of the rhythm that comes through a drama: "one [type of time] . . . is hustle and bustle, and the other the feeling for that deeper movement of human life that leads into something great" *CA* 45.

71. *IF* 141, 138-39.

chooses to live the faith as it moves a person through the finite to a sense of the infinite.[72]

1. The Childhood Stage: The initial stage of faith is characterized by all the uneducated reachings of primal faith. The faith of the child is absolute and clear. The world is neatly divided into the good and the bad. Absolutes come easily. Either one's father is all-powerful or he has no power at all. Univocal "either-or" thinking is in full operation as this childhood faith sorts out the experiences of this life. The inner life of the child offers a sort of playground where absolute, unconditioned autonomous wishes construct a world much to the liking of the child.[73]

At this very important and delicate stage, a child needs assistance in constructing and maintaining images that help the child in contacting objects happily. Illusions can provide a creative and gentle way to engage the world. Lynch notes that this will work only if someone is willing to enter into collusion with the faith of the child. However, one of life's chief tasks at this stage is to begin to surrender those illusions gradually in order to adjust to the autonomy of the world. Otherwise, a child will contact only its inadequate images while reality presents itself as one frustration after another.[74]

During this first stage, a rather vague, unspoken promise becomes an operative dynamic in life. The womb of the mother, her warm caresses, the satisfying meals, the endless attention, and

72. Lynch was well aware of Erik Erikson's work on the stages of the life cycle. See *IH* 273, *IF* 121. I have not discovered any evidence that Lynch was aware of James Fowler's work, although Fowler makes use of Lynch's *Images of Faith* several times in his *Stages of Faith* (New York: Harper and Row, 1981), 36, 105, 115, 211, 212.

73. *IF* 111.

74. *IF* 63, 118. This childhood stage dies hard in the lives of many. Although this stage of faith is proper to children, perhaps it might be called the "absolute" or "univocal" stage of faith, since it can be found in large groups of adults as well. In its adult forms, it seems to thrive on the ability to abstract something from actual existence and then call it God. Unfortunately, this leaves the believer with only a "ghost at the end of the process." Lynch suggested that even a nation's culture may be marred with tinges of this first stage. For example, he credited Cervantes' *Don Quixote* with having achieved for Spain an advance from this romantic type of faith. *IF* 121-23.

so forth, give credence to the fulfillment of a promise of easy living. A primal faith arises in relation to that promise, which soon gives rise to a series of expectations, some more reasonable than others.[75]

2. The Unexpected Stage of Faith: At the second stage, after a period of some disappointment, the believer does not abandon the promise, but rather begins to verify the promise and look for evidence. This period tests the believer's ability to live in anticipation as renewals of the promise are sought.

At this point, the believer is called upon to reconcile the promise, the faith, and the facts. Expectations need to be adjusted in view of the unexpected. Yet the expected and the unexpected need to be kept together in a creative way so that one does not destroy the other. In fact, the unexpected may even be seen as fulfilling the expected. Thus the believer tastes irony and needs to develop an analogical imagination that can handle both the expected and the unexpected dimensions of faith. In this stage of faith, the promise becomes clarified only as it reaches fulfillment. As the promise of the Resurrection meets our awareness of the inevitability of death, a gap is perceived. Both ends of the gap must be held together in the imaginative act of faith. That act requires energy, but our willingness to continue expecting, even though we have encountered the unexpected, sustains the energy for that act of faith.[76]

3. The Building a Present Moment Stage: Once the ironic dimension of faith has been grasped, the believer is free to develop faith in the present rather than to consider faith as an effort prompting an escape from the present. The believer is called to extend the sense of irony into the dimension of time.[77]

If time is simply cast aside in favor of a formless eternity, then self-destructive apocalyptic images result. A belief in the dead begins to occupy center stage. Fantastic images then imitate faith in their ability to sustain belief and project a future. The

---

75. *IF* 125-6, 112.
76. *IF* 112, 130-31.
77. *IF* 132.

present and what it can accomplish are rejected. It is too "ordinary" to be of any use. Instead, the spectacular is sought.[78]

To build a present moment, the believer must have the help of the past and future. Only those who are aware of the relevant past are in a position to assess correctly the present moment. Only those who can look to a world of promise and possibility in the future can give creative direction to the present that is "not only fact but fact and possibility." Faith does not reject the present. It creates it with "the help of what was and what will be."[79]

4. The Movement through Infinite Possibility Stage: At this stage, the believer is confronted with the overwhelming variety of possibilities that exist both for good and for evil. We have reached a level of technical competence that not only allows unprecedented exploration and use of outer space, but also of our "inner space" given the advances in the fields of genetic engineering and the psychiatric sciences.[80]

Real choices must be made in the course of our evolutionary development, yet there is no blueprint or plan to follow. A totally rational God would be quite limited. But a God who is aware of the nature of dilemmas (that can have no satisfying answer) and tragedies, and can suffer them is truly an unlimited, free God. Drawing an example from Dostoevsky's *Brothers Karamazov*, Lynch recalls the story of a boy who had injured one of the general's hounds. As punishment, the general sent the hounds after the boy. They tore him to pieces before his mother's eyes. A simplistic image of harmony in which "everything works for the best" cannot explain such a story. Every possibility cannot simply produce harmony. Faith does not begin in serenity, it moves into serenity with the production of images that respond more fully to reality each step of the way. Here, one needs faith that can assure a person that the overwhelming nature of infinite possibility can be controlled by Providence and promise working in concert.[81]

---

78. *IF* 133.
79. *IF* 134-35.
80. *IF* 144-45.
81. *IF* 147, 152.

5. The Passage through the Curse Stage: At this stage, the believer focuses on "the curse," a factor that has been present throughout all the stages, but now calls for specific attention. Simply stated, the curse existed once, but it exists no longer because Jesus took it upon himself. But the consequences of the curse remain. The consequences of the curse consist of those many forms of letting go that tempt a person to think that life is merely a tease. One enjoys a taste of life, a taste of love, but then they are taken away. Sorrow, suffering, illness, death, separation, poverty, grief, etc., constitute consequences of the curse. Through the ironic transformation of faith, the curses are transformed into blessings. Keeping the elements of blessing and curse together now becomes a task for the imagination.

Lynch assures us that "redemption is there but must be received and imagined." Redemption is not automatic. To receive it, we need to imagine it in some form. The imagination of faith must become fully operative because "the promises are achieved through the very conditions of the curse." In a sense, if it cannot be imagined, it cannot be transformed. If it cannot be transformed, it cannot be saved. The challenge here is to embrace the weakness and the commonness – the human that must die – and to give those elements affectionate redemptive images. Such are the images of the Beatitudes that declare the poor, the hungry, the mourning, and the despised to be blessed, and foretell of their transformations.[82]

6. The Tragic Stage: Perhaps the most difficult stage in faith brings us to a realization of the tragic dimension of human reality. Particularly if our movement through the infinite possibility stage has been imperfect and if our passage through the curse has been tinged with a hatred of our own weakness, then the stage in which the tragic dimension of life moves into prominence will cause problems.

Often believers assume that faith is not tragic and that everything works out in the end. However, when death strikes not as a tragedy that happens to someone else, but as a personal

---

82. *IF* 159-61.

reality that threatens one's own life, then the believer's glib aphorisms about immortality and resurrection are subjected to a searching reexamination. If death is real, and if the Christian is expected to follow Christ into the grave, then we need to expect really to die. We need to be willing to embrace a point of complete helplessness, the end of all energy. The point of death has already been foretold in life through the many "forms of the mortalities of human sensibility: failure, shame, . . . the coming to a truth that is the dropping of a mask, the coming into the range of human pain, sorrow, and solitude." At this most difficult juncture, Lynch does not hold back. Even though believers may speak of death as a beginning, and properly so, they must face up to the same reality everyone else faces. Lynch hypothesized that "the dead man can do nothing, absolutely nothing." In that sense, death introduces a "factor of absolute nothingness" that is "at its center."[83] Now according to Lynch's metaphysics, there is no such thing as "absolute nothingness," but there is a relative nothingness that resides within the heart of being. As our relative being is reduced to relative nothingness, that nothingness is still related to Being in some way. Our faith suggests that it is related ironically to Being so that our nonbeing allows the fullness of Being free ground in which to play out an irony that is reflected in the Resurrection.

If Lynch is correct in his assertion that faithfulness to the infinite demands faithfulness to the finite, then believers are called to taste their finitude to the very end. True death is part of that finitude. Faith "is the grace to give in to this ending, this weakness, this nothingness." That is a mark of its peace. Faith does not deny the tragic – it deepens it. Faith plunges into the finite. But here the deepest irony begins. Here death reveals itself as the first cousin of love. Both must "give in" completely to reach perfection. The emptiness of death ironically reflects the fullness of love.[84]

7. *The Death and Nothingness Stage:* The contemplation of death and the experience of death itself are two different things. Hence,

---

83. *IF* 164, 167.
84. *IF* 167-88.

they form two different stages in the life of faith. Like faith, death is simple, yet not so simple. Everyone must die. It will be accomplished. Yet it is not so simple. Each of us may be faced with an agony in the garden as death approaches on a personal and immediate level.

Lynch warns that such a struggle will be increased in an unproductive way if we expect not to die completely, but to reach a state in which we are only half-dead. The problem with this notion, as Lynch notes, is that it saddles us with the impossible burden of not dying, of holding on to something rather than letting go. This does not mean that we should not struggle to live, for example, to defeat a life-threatening illness. But when death finally occurs, we should not expect to avoid the taste of mortality. Faith teaches precisely the opposite. "This point [death] is not destroyed or taken away by faith, but used."[85]

Faith at death has the same structure as hope and love. The hopeful Christian does not annihilate human weakness. The weakness becomes an arena of God's activity. Weakness ironically creates its opposite. So too with love. Its self-emptying activity ironically reveals itself to be the very vehicle of its fullness. The nonbeing of death also attracts its opposite. While some moderns accept the nothingness of death but consider it absurd, the faithful see death as the final nothingness that is productive in the hands of God.[86]

If faith is not less tragic than usually imagined, but more tragic, then it is also true to say that it is more ironic than is usually imagined. Lynch claimed that faith always reaches for the right taste of reality. It is not simply the bitter taste of horror, nor is it the sweet taste of the "the decadent romantics." The taste of faith needs to retain the bittersweet taste of an ironic Christic imagination that can hold opposites together without giving in to a cynical despair nor to a glib presumptuousness that blinds us to the tragic dimension of faith. Faith, rather, is to be sustained in Christic hope.[87]

---

85. *IF* 169.
86. *IF* 169-72.
87. *IF* 173-74. Lynch's thoughts on death are similar to Karl Rahner's. Both saw deep irony in death. Both claimed that death brings both "fulfillment and emptiness." Karl Rahner, *On the Theology of Death*, trans. C. Henkey (New

V. Faith's Grammar of Ascent

Early on in the course of the *Scarlet Letter*, Roger Chillingworth, Hester's anonymous legal husband, returns not to claim Hester as his wife but to torment the secretive Reverend Arthur Dimmesdale, Hester's well-respected anonymous paramour.

The "tooth of guilt" having gnawed at his heart for seven years, the sickly Arthur one day leaves the festive Election Day parade amid its music and laughter to claim Hester and her child. Together, to the dismay of the crowd, they ascend the scaffold. As Arthur submits to his humiliation in the ascent, Chillingworth declares that Arthur's escape from him could occur only on that scaffold at the most public of times and places. As Hester Prynne's humiliation was her exaltation, so too with Arthur Dimmesdale. In the acceptance of the curse, he discovered freedom. The scaffold was the cross that set him free.

It was there on the scaffold that the sickly Dimmesdale gave in to death. At that moment, Hester suggested that perhaps they would be able to spend eternity together. Although the possibility could not be dismissed, Arthur refused to presume upon a future in which everything works out for the best:

> "Hush, Hester, hush! . . . It may be, that, when we forgot our God, – when we violated our reverence for each other's soul, – it was thenceforth vain to hope that we could meet hereafter, in an everlasting pure reunion. God knows, and He is merciful! He hath proved his mercy most of all in my afflictions. . . . Had . . . these agonies been wanting, I would have been lost forever!"[88]

Years later Hester returned to the town and resumed wearing the scarlet letter. That letter had "long since ceased to be a stigma which attracted the world's scorn and bitterness, . . . [it] became

York: Herder and Herder, 1972), 40. However, Rahner at one point developed the traditional images in terms that posit an immediate, continuing, postdeath "pancosmic" relationship of a soul to the world. Lynch seemed to be more skeptical about whether Christian images communicate the metaphysical structure of death. Such images rather communicate the fact of hope, not the way in which such hope is eventually realized.

88. Hawthorne, *The Scarlet Letter*, chap. 23, p. 181.

a type of something to be sorrowed over, and looked upon with awe, yet with reverence too."[89]

Such is the bittersweet taste of faith. It ironically flourishes in weakness. It has its moments of joy but accepts its moments of grief. Faith establishes our identity, our heart, as we use its images as a path to other hearts as well. Then, as paths cross, we hope the light of faith will reveal unexpectedly a merciful God as well. Sometimes faith is a comfort and a joy. At other times, like the scarlet letter, faith is also "something to be sorrowed over, and looked upon with awe, yet with reverence too." Faith's ironic Christic transformations give the believer confidence to hope in God's mercy so that today's sweet joys that give way to the tomorrow's bitter sorrows may prefigure the Eighth Day's mystery of triumphant Paschal love. The way up is through our humble assent to the weakness of our finitude. The way up is discovered only in the way down. Faith is not only a free assent of the mind and will, but, perhaps more profoundly, it is a free ironic ascent of life through one's descent into life's frailties. Such is faith's ironic grammar of ascent.

---

89. Ibid., p. 185.

CHAPTER FOUR

Conclusion:
Exploring a Paradigm Shift

THE LAST ANYONE HEARD OF ICHABOD CRANE, HE HAD UNSUCCESSFULLY attempted to dodge a pumpkin head hurled at him just as he crossed the church bridge in his escape from the headless horseman of Sleepy Hollow. Washington Irving tells us that he left nothing behind but a small bundle of odds and ends, including a dog-eared book of psalm tunes and a broken pitch pipe.

These remains were subtle reminders of Ichabod's fertile imagination, which was so stirred by the sounds of nature at dusk that he would sing the psalms "either to drown thought or drive away the spirits." Though he was noted for his singing of the psalmody, perhaps an unbroken pitch pipe would have assisted this hapless believer in his attempt to deal with God's word at the right pitch. Ichabod should not be counted as the only unfortunate soul with such propensities. Anyone who enters that sleepy region, Irving writes, may ". . . inhale the witching influence of the air, and begin to grow imaginative – to dream dreams and see apparitions."[1]

Does the act of faith result in a people who only dream dreams and see apparitions? Throughout the course of our journey, we have entered the Sleepy Hollows of faith in an effort to assess the legitimacy of the act of faith. Under the guidance of William Lynch, we have attempted to view imagination in positive

---

1. Washington Irving, "The Legend of Sleepy Hollow," 335, 331.

terms to appreciate its role in putting us in touch with reality. Yet there remains the possibility, fully recognized by Lynch, that the imagination may run rampant, and with it, not only faith but reason as well. When the theological pitch pipe breaks, even Scripture may be used to drown out thought and to invite obsessions about phantoms that are only the projections of our own fears.

In their eagerness to protect the faithful from the allegations of the rationalists, fideists, atheists, and others, some Scholastic theologians proposed a faith that was supposedly objective without also being subjective. To be subjective was to be false. To be imaginative was to depart from the real.[2] As progress was made .in the recovery of the original works of St. Thomas, theologians like Rousselot, Maréchal, the Rahner brothers, Lonergan, and others began to break with customary Scholastic strategies. It was time for a closer look at modernity's concern for the subjective validity of the act of faith.

In that turn to the subject, we find the beginnings of a paradigm shift in the notion of faith. We will discuss Lynch's contribution to theology as it furthered of that paradigm shift. Lynch pays attention not only to the subjective notion of the primordial will, as Blondel had already done, but also attempts to include every facet of the human by featuring the ironic Christic imagination as central to the act of faith. Consideration will also be given to Carlos Cirne-Lima's attempt to form a bridge between the Scholastic notions of faith and the modern notions. Cirne-Lima's thought will give rise to some indication of the place of Lynch's contribution to the theological discussion on faith. Finally, the practical implications of Lynch's contributions will be noted as they relate to today's pastoral setting.

---

2. Although Scholastics recognized the foundational importance of the phantasm when the intellect abstracts from the image to produce the concept, they drew sharp distinctions between thought and imagination, and seemed to be thoroughly disinterested in investigating the continuing positive role the imagination plays in the process of faith and reason. See R. Garrigou-Lagrange, *Reality: A Synthesis of Thomistic Thought*, trans. P. Cummins (St. Louis: B. Herder, 1950) 179-80; and Cardinal Mercier, *A Manual of Modern Scholastic Philosophy*, vol. 1, (St. Louis: B. Herder, 1932), 211.

I. Paradigms in Theology

As it is used here, a paradigm simply means what Hans Küng described as an "interpretive model," an "explanatory model," or "models for understanding." Drawing from Thomas Kuhn's definition, Küng considers a paradigm as "an entire constellation of beliefs, values, techniques, and so on, shared by the members of a given community."[3] A paradigm tacitly defines the parameters of legitimate discussion, determining what is relevant to the concept under consideration. It exists by way of assumption in order to deal with the facts that are encountered, and it is always indirectly present.

For example, when faith is mentioned, many would not bat an eyelash if the discussion were carried on in terms of belief. But belief is only one of many different possible expressions of faith. If the discussion began to include the notions of trust, ultimate concern, and an attitude of dependence, people would generally have little problem in following along. Indeed, people generally have little problem in understanding the distinction between "faith," which would denote a person's basic orientation, their openness to the divine, and "belief," which would designate an acceptance of an intellectually formulated assertion of what is true in light of the faith that one has adopted.

Now interject the notion of faith as imagination. Eyebrows are raised and foreheads are furrowed. Explanations are required. Imagination is generally not considered to be legitimately related to faith. To the common mind, it elicits notions of fantasy and illusion, and, therefore, imagination is generally not accepted as part of the paradigm for faith.

To the literary mind, however, the imagination has a more respectable history. It has been considered as an indispensable instrument by which we can pierce the surfaces of reality. It is by virtue of the imagination that things can be perceived as having not only presence, but meaning. The dozen roses that a husband

---

3. Hans Küng, "Paradigm Change in Theology: A Proposal for Discussion," in *Paradigm Change in Theology*, ed. Hans Küng and David Tracy (New York: Crossroad, 1989), 7, 9. See Thomas Kuhn, *The Structure of Scientific Revolutions*, 2nd ed. (Chicago: University of Chicago Press, 1970), 175.

brings home have more than a botanical significance to his wife. They have a poetic significance as well – by far the more important meaning. How is it that the wife may validly interpret those flowers as a sign of love? It is by means of her poetic imagination. In other words, she has exercised "faith" in her husband. By that faith, husband and wife both discover and create their love. That is, they discover and create each other. The poetic dimension of their lives creates and discovers symbols by which their experience may be expressed, reinforced, and created anew in the context of their faith in each other. Their love is not the "same old love" with which they began their marriage. It is deeper, more profound, and even brand-new by virtue of the ability of the poetic imagination to redescribe and recreate that reality. It is in that sense that Lynch would have us conceive of faith as imagination.

Our relationship with God depends on our ability to perceive divine meaning in the creation in which we live. That divine meaning is a divine presence. It is a grace. But that grace is not apparent to all. It does not lie on the surface of finite reality. It is not simply immanent. We need the divine light of faith to see it. We need a poetic imagination powerful enough to perceive if only indirectly the divine stamp on creation. That is to say, a reflection of the divine transcendence is found within the very immanence of this world.

Discussion of faith as imagination assumes a different paradigm for faith than the older Scholastic intellectualist model. It represents a shift, but not a departure. When a paradigm shift occurs, we do not drop all associations with the previous paradigm, and begin with a completely different set of definitions and relationships. A paradigm shift in the theological context involves a sublation. That is, previous concepts are included but exceeded. A higher viewpoint is attained, and previous concepts can be seen in new relationships with other concepts that had previously been thought to be outside the purview of discussion.[4]

---

4. Hans Küng, "Paradigm Change in Theology: A Proposal for Discussion," and Norbert Greinacher, "What Must Be Born in Mind in a New Paradigm," in *Paradigm Change in Theology: A Symposium for the Future*, ed. H. Küng and D. Tracy (New York: Crossroad, 1989), 7, 227.

Moreover, in a true paradigm shift, it seems that the center of gravity shifts. What had previously been considered of central importance, carrying decisive weight, is now superseded by other factors that are thought to carry more fundamental significance. The old paradigm is no longer thought to be a completely balanced view of things. Adjustments must be made throughout the paradigm. In other words, in a paradigm shift, the higher viewpoint yields not only a more encompassing view of the periphery or the edges of a topic. It also shifts the center of attention, and with that shift, other areas of the paradigm are seen from a new angle.

A paradigm shift thus represents a sublation in which the center of gravity has shifted. The paradigm shift is related to previous paradigms, but the new paradigm offers a true change that is worthy of our attention. For example, when faith is discussed, Lynch would certainly be comfortable in discussing the intellectualist concerns of belief, but he would not think that the most fundamental elements of faith had thereby been treated. A paradigm shift would be required to reach adequately those more profound levels.

II. A Paradigm Bridge

In moving from the Scholastic to the Modern paradigm, a movement that is yet to be completed, there have been a number of theologians who have managed to display some ease in operating within either paradigm. Cardinal Victor Dechamps, John Henry Newman, Maurice Blondel, Pierre Rousselot, Joseph Maréchal, and others have displayed that talent. One of Karl Rahner's Brazilian students, Carlos Cirne-Lima, possessed such a talent, and focused on building a bridge between the two paradigms specifically in terms of faith.[5]

---

5. Unknown to Cirne-Lima at the time, Bernard Lonergan had published similar findings in a series of articles that did not, however, specifically focus on the act of faith. The articles are collected in *Verbum: Word and Idea in Aquinas*, ed. D. Burrell (Notre Dame: University of Notre Dame Press, 1967).

In his book, *Personal Faith*, Cirne-Lima begins with a brief phenomenological treatment of faith to place it in a personal context. That is, the object of faith is primarily a person, not merely a proposition. Now this "object," or person, is first encountered by us through our ability to form an intuition of that person, or, in other words, through our ability to form a personal image.[6]

Cirne-Lima cautions us that an intuition is "prepredicative." It is simply given. It is not yet a sentence, and, therefore, no judgment is involved. One merely grasps the object and does not attempt comparisons with other intuitions or concepts. The intellect takes intuitions as self-disclosures of reality. As such, those self-disclosures can be considered as "evidence." Intuition gives a person an image to "look into" with the mind's eye, not merely the sensible eye. It forms the source of our concepts, judgments, and syllogisms. Intuition gives rise to discursive thought, which then may be used to analyze and judge those intuitions in order to prepare ourselves to have more acute intuitions of reality in the future.[7]

In order to know someone as a person, not merely as an impersonal object, an act of free knowledge is required. It is an act of knowledge because the understanding is involved. It is an act of freedom because it requires a choice to be "with" the other, not merely "next to" the other. When a person makes a free decision to be with another, the whole person in an attitude of openness is present to the other who is also in an attitude of openness.

The intuition that emerges from a personal encounter has access to the deeper realms of the other person whose self-disclosures result in a more or less perfect intuitive cognition depending on whether that person wants to endure the vulner-

---

6. Carlos Cirne-Lima, *Personal Faith: A Metaphysical Inquiry*, trans. G. R. Dimler (New York: Herder and Herder, 1965), 69-72, 78-79, 93. Hereinafter cited as "*PF*." This discussion may prove to be exasperating for poststructuralists who have become so enamored of texts that they seem to have lost confidence in any referent beyond the text. John Searle has proposed correctives, including a defense of a version of the correspondence theory of truth that would allow philosophers to regain some confidence in speaking once again of reality. See his book, *The Construction of Social Reality*, supra.

7. *PF* 80, 85, 90-91, 95, 102-3.

ability of being known. What is known of the other as a person largely depends on the mutual love and trust that arise between the knower and the known. The "evidences" or "intuitions" that result are of a higher order than the intuitions of nonpersonal knowledge because personal knowledge gains access to the unseen "inside" of a person that can never become an "outside" without that person's willing it.[8]

Personal faith and personal knowledge are the same thing. When personal *faith* is the issue, we focus on the free aspect of love in those personal intuitions. When personal *knowledge* is the issue, we focus on what we know as a result of encountering that person in love. Hence, the object of both personal knowledge and faith is the "Thou" whom we love.[9] The substance of faith consists in the contents of the intuitions that come from the object of faith as a result of the act of love.

Since the substance of faith subsists at the intuitive, prediscursive level of personal knowledge, the Scholastic notion of truth as the conformity of the intellect to the thing is not completely satisfactory.[10] The substance of personal knowledge includes intuitive knowledge, but adds the dimension of the freely posited relationship.[11] Thus personal knowledge retains an intuitive or

---

8. *PF* 114, 129-30.

9. *PF* 136. This approach is reflected in Lonergan when he defined faith as "the knowledge born of religious love." *Method in Theology* (New York: Seabury, 1972), 115.

10. *PF* 138. Cirne-Lima claims that the intuition is automatically aware of its adequacy. It is formal truth. It is "evidence." He therefore defines intuitive truth as the conformity of the intellect to the thing insofar as the intellect sees to be what is. "Veritas intuitionis est adaequatio intellectus et rei, quatenus intellectus videt esse, quod est." Even if the intuition is a hallucination, it is a seeing to be what is. "What is" in that case would be the hallucination. The difficulty comes, of course, in our judgment. Yet Cirne-Lima claims that the intuition is aware of its own adequation to reality. One might object that Cirne-Lima has at this point made the intuition into a predicative act. That is, it now appears to be involved in making judgments of adequacy. Nevertheless, there is some validity in his thought insofar as he is claiming that our judgment will concern ultimately an intuition that carries our experience of reality with it, not ultimately a concept that is merely an abstraction from an intuition. *PF* 141.

11. Hence, Cirne-Lima claims that the truth of personal knowledge is the conformity of the intellect to the thing insofar as the intellect partly sees to be what is, and partly voluntarily places it to be that way so that it might come

receptive aspect, and an attitudinal or projective aspect. All this occurs at a level of intuitive immediacy. That is, it is mediated by the image that is intuited. The substance of faith is prior to conceptual analysis and comparative judgments. Once those concepts and judgments are made, a secondary discursive level of knowledge is posited, which can lead to further, more perfect encounters in personal knowledge or to a loss of faith and a withdrawal.

Cirne-Lima then considers some typically Scholastic interests such as the concerns over evidences, certitude, the analysis of faith, and credibility. The certitude of personal faith is found right within the act of faith itself. Faith is not based on a certitude, rather, certitude (when it comes) is based on faith. The contents of the personal intuition constitute the evidence that gives rise to certitude. One is consciously aware of the contents of the intuition as "evidence." To ask for evidence of its truth is impertinent. There is no such thing as evidence for evidence. Either something is taken as evident, or it is not. There can be no infinite regress to see what "backs up" the evidence as if one were examining the logical chain of a syllogism. We cannot leave our experience of something to see what backs up that experience.[12]

---

to be. "Adaequatio intellectus et rei, quatenus intellectus (cum voluntate) ponit esse ita, ut fiat." *PF* 144.

12. *PF* 153. However, evidence may be critiqued in terms of other evidence or in terms of alternative ways of looking at the issue under investigation. We may come across a piece of information that does not "fit" with what we have taken to be evident up to that point. Then we have uncovered an anomaly that might be left aside until a suitable explanation occurs to someone. Alternatively, we might consider that what was formerly a piece of evidence has lost its intelligibility as evidence for that particular view of things. New evidence might suggest a new theory. A man might think he sees a pebble. He might then walk a few paces to the side, and it might appear to be a leaf. He might inspect it more closely and confirm for himself that it is in fact a leaf. The man has considered together three separate experiences. He has not "gone behind" any of the experiences that were taken as evidence when he had them. He might then return to his first position and have a different experience of that leaf than he had at first. Cirne-Lima is correct in claiming that there is no such thing as evidence for evidence, but there is the possibility of a collateral critique of evidence by considering how it coheres with, or makes sense along with, other pieces of information. Hence, there is no infinite regress, but an infinite expanse that "evidence" seeks to tie together. Thus, a theory either holds together or it does not.

Although personal faith is ontologically dependent on the image, it is not logically dependent on anything but itself. In other words, personal faith assumes something to believe in. It assumes an intuition, but there is no logical source for the certitude other than the contents that were intuited. Those contents were made possible by the free commitment of love that was made to the other person. That is to say that personal knowledge, or faith, is self-motivated. It discovers its ground in the relationship itself. The grounds of faith are not extrinsic to the believer, but intrinsic.[13]

Supernatural faith differs from natural faith in its divine object. For the Christian, faith is placed in God through the "yes" that is spoken to Jesus Christ. The image or intuition of Christ is mediated to the Christian through those who proclaim his gospel. That image of Christ as the perfect human faithfully performing God's mission is either received as certain (at least to some degree) or it is rejected.[14]

The formation of this intuition as worthy of belief is the same phenomenon that Scholastics called the judgment of credibility. But there is no consideration of the preambles of faith in a detached, neutral setting. As we encounter the evidences of faith, they carry some credibility or they do not. It all comes together in the intuition. At the end of a discursive thought process, one might reflect again on the initial intuition and might see more grounds for faith or perhaps reason to doubt. Additional faith experiences will be strengthened or weakened as the intuitive sense is sharpened with respect to the perfection or lack of perfection of the object of faith.[15] The openness required in

---

13. *PF* 160, 162, 153, 166, 197-98, 201. Furthermore, the certitude of faith will vary according to the person who is the object of faith. Cirna-Lima explains that we might have a very penetrating intuition of a person who should not be trusted. Faith in that person will be low. On the other hand, a lesser intuition of a particularly virtuous person can produce a much deeper faith. *PF* 166-167.

14. *PF* 199, 202. We prescind here from the complex task of relating the Christian faith to the faith of other world religions. Lynch would refine this notion that one either believes or does not. Faith and fear are often found together. See *IF* 91.

15. Hence, Cirna-Lima is not faced with the technical problem of the "analysis of faith." The certitude of faith that is greater than any of its preambles is a problem only if the evidences of faith are considered as extrinsic to the act of

the personal relationship of faith yields "insider" knowledge that is denied to those who merely look on as neutral observers.

Cirna-Lima's views attempt to form a bridge from the Scholastic to the modern paradigm. He accepts the epistemological categories of St. Thomas, thereby inviting Scholastic interest in his theory, but he elaborates the object of faith in terms of a personal relationship, thereby integrating insights from the modern paradigms, an object that is considerably more complex than mere propositional belief, which Scholastics were accustomed to treating as the equivalent of faith. The intellectualist concern for belief is important and necessary, but it is not primary. Before one arrives at a notion of faith as belief in the statements of another, the more fundamental aspects of personal faith must be handled.

One might conclude from Cirne-Lima's thoughts that it makes more sense to speak of the certitude of beliefs that are based on faith than to speak of the certitude of faith. As Cirne-Lima contends, if the substance of faith is contained in the intuition, then faith is prepredicative. It is prior to any judgment. Certitude should come as the result of a reflection on one's faith. Faith concerns truth. If one's faith has led to more reliable dealings with reality, if it has led one to more insightful dealings with the world, that person will find more grounds for certitude. On the other hand, if faith has betrayed the unwary believer, if it has led to a fantasy that must be adjusted as it bumps up against the harsh realities of life, that person will find reasons to nurture doubt. This approach would draw support from Lynch's observation that faith is a way of collecting and fashioning the evidence. It is the broader worldview within which beliefs arise. Faith can be more or less adequate, coherent, or fruitful, in which case true beliefs about the relationship will arise. Or faith can be inadequate,

---

faith itself. The Scholastic syllogism assumed that the evidences for faith were equally available for all to see. One had only to inspect them as a detached neutral observer to reach the conclusion that faith ought to be placed in God through the grace of Jesus Christ as it has been extended to us through the Catholic Church. Cirne-Lima challenges that deductive certitude by noting that the evidence for faith is found in an accepted relationship where the evidence is not complete apart from the operation of the will. *PF* 196-97, 203.

incoherent, and barren, in which case false beliefs will be nurtured.

Although Lynch called this intuitive dimension the "center of faith," he did not call it the whole of faith. Lynch cautioned us that although it is helpful to distinguish faith and belief, it is important to avoid their total separation. Both Lynch and Cirne-Lima consider the intuitive aspects of faith as primary, but not to the exclusion of the notion of faith as belief.

Both Lynch and Cirne-Lima include that "central core" of faith, but it must be noted that when Lynch considers faith as imagination, his conception of the imagination is much broader than Cirne-Lima's notion of personal intuition. Lynch does not feel constrained to limit "faith" to that mysterious central intuition that puts reality together. He cautions us that "there is a real possibility that by any confinement of faith to the center we may be doing grave injustice to the center itself." We must also look to its periphery, "where faith comes out as a highly developed construct of character, sensibility, judgments, images, reactions." For Lynch, the imagination not only receives the images by which we encounter personal reality, the imagination also plays with that reality's image quite deliberately at times. The imagination teases us through its images. It prompts us "to think more," as Ricoeur would say. Recall that for Lynch faith as imagination includes all those resources by which a person encounters the concrete world to form images of the world "to find it, cope with it, shape it, even to make it."[16] Moreover, all these conscious decisions do not happen only in an individual's personal intuition. For Lynch, faith as imagination is communal.

For example, a person might hit upon a dramatic image that will deepen our notion of what it means to love. But the image has not yet been posited in the concrete. First the arduous work of the playwright must be done. There are many judgments, acts of reflection, and acts of "sympathetic imagination" that might take place, none of which can be reduced to the immediacy of

---

16. Paul Ricoeur, "Herméneutique de l'idée de Révélation," in *La Révélation*, ed. P. Ricoeur (Bruxelles: Facultés universitaires Saintes-Louis, 1977), 21. *IF* 64-65; *CP* 23.

the intuition that receives an image in the sense in which Cirne-Lima intends. By the time the drama is performed, the conscious efforts of a whole company of actors, actresses, stage-hands, and many others have contributed to the performance of the image of the drama. Yet this drama is an act of the imagination, not only the intuition, and the resulting play is an image that can embody the faith. The play itself is an act of faith, not in spite of, but because of the fact that it is an act of the imagination that includes many judgments, conceptions, trials, errors, rational analyses, adjustments, and readjustments. Furthermore, as the play takes hold of our imaginations, it "plays" us. As Ricoeur would say, it proposes a world in which we might dwell for a while. We might then judge that the image is worthy of being integrated into our everyday operating view of reality. We might use it as a model in our dealings with others. In Ricoeur's words, we might well "appropriate" the image. That too is an act of faith.[17]

It follows that Lynch extends "faith" into the arena where judgments are made and beliefs are adopted. There is some real sense in making this extension. The Church has long held that Christian faith requires belief in a historically embodied Jesus. Such a belief must be the result of a judgment. If faith were *only* intuition, such a fundamental holding could not distinguish faith in a historical Jesus from faith in an archetype. The Catholic faith demands more than belief in an archetype. Therefore, such faith must extend to the arena of our beliefs.

Hence, Lynch's theology is not inimical to the themes of Scholastic theology insofar as it attempts to offer a rational rendition of faith as belief. He merely sees the Scholastic project as somewhat truncated and dated. His development of the idea

---

17. Appropriation, for Ricoeur, makes what is initially alien as one's own. It "actualizes the meaning of the text for the present reader." This happens as a person "plays" with the text. Ricoeur cautions us that "whoever plays is also played. . . ." To enter into play with a text, "one must divest oneself of the earlier 'me' in order to receive, as in play, the self conferred by the work itself." Paul Ricoeur, *Hermeneutics and the Human Sciences: Essays on Language, Action and Interpretation*, trans. J. B. Thompson (New Haven: Yale University Press, 1970), 185-86, 190-92. Ricoeur acknowledges the work of Hans-Georg Gadamer, especially in the development of the metaphor of play.

of faith as imagination attempts to bring faith and belief into their modern context.

III. The Paradigm Shifts

Lynch's theological proposals are not mere window dressing. They do shift our attention from the Scholastic paradigm in ways that open new avenues in our thought about faith. Some of the more important shifts that occur with the adoption of this paradigm should be enumerated. In other words, if believers choose to cross the paradigm bridge, where will they find themselves?

First, whereas the Scholastics proposed that faith is addressed to the intellect and will, Lynch sees faith as addressed to the imagination. For Scholastics, the act of faith came when the will directed the intellect to believe a given proposition. For Lynch, faith lies at a deeper level than the propositional. Faith refers to the imaginative framework by which believers experience life in a certain way. Faith as imagination informs their entire world of experiencing (loving, willing, thinking, choosing, seeing, etc.), not just the intellectual aspect of the world.

Second, whereas the Scholastics treated the evidences of faith as "pure," Lynch asserts that faith composes, discovers, and creates its evidence. Operating within a classical worldview, Scholastics thought it obvious that the evidence for faith was "pure," uninterpreted, available for all to see quite plainly. For Lynch, the way one sees the evidence is precisely the faith that is being employed. In the act of faith, people accept their position in the "whole" that the "One" has given to believers who are the "many." For Scholastic theologians, grace was always considered essential for faith, but they experienced some difficulty in explaining why. For Lynch, it is of the essence because grace describes the relationship between the One and the many.

Third, for Scholastics there was only one rationality, one way of assembling the facts for believer and infidel alike. Therefore, a rational certitude could be achieved. Lynch rejected the notion of a univocal rationality. He saw faith as the paradigmatic imagination. As we adopt an image or a set of images, we also adopt the rationality appropriate to those images. That rationality will be different from the rationality expressed in competing images. Once we are committed to an image, there are a whole series of commitments that follow, not the least of which is its way of thinking.

Fourth, for some of the Scholastics faith tended to be a rather presumptuous act. After all, especially for some, like Billot and Bainvel, faith could be proven, and, even though that act of proof would not be necessarily equivalent to an act of faith, one could adhere to various doctrines with the knowledge that intellectual certitude could be achieved. For Lynch, faith is always a humble act. It operates through the logic of irony which so often leaves us in a posture of hope, not presumption. Lacking all things, can we truly find a treasure? Can we find new life through death? That is not only our faith, that is our hope. There is a certitude involved in faith, but it is not derived from a deductive formal logic that so easily gives rise to presumption.

Fifth, Scholastics viewed evidence as extrinsic to the life of the believer. It appeared that a mystery such as the Resurrection was used primarily as an event that furnished the authority to back up various propositions. It almost seems as though the Resurrection could have been replaced by any other miracle. It was used to show that Jesus had divine authority. Whatever he said, therefore, must be true, and whomever he authorized must be trustworthy. Lynch, on the other hand, sees the evidences of faith as intrinsic to the life of the believer. The ironic Christic imagination composes that evidence, and it sees in the very real event of the Resurrection the most forceful instance of the content of revelation itself. Here the irony of faith is pushed to the limit. The lowly one, the humiliated one, the dead one has been exalted. He is risen. It does not back up other messages. That *is* the message in light of which every other message, every other experience, is interpreted. When we "catch on" to the way of the cross, which is the way of the Risen One, faith begins to be lived from the inside. Then propositions can be developed as worthwhile and important guides.

Sixth, Scholastics viewed faith and belief on the same level. Bainvel defined faith as belief in the testimony of another. For

Lynch, faith subsists at a deeper level than beliefs. Faith constitutes the most general context, our way of experiencing, and, in view of that context, a content that is viewed in a way that is different from those who profess a different faith. That content can, more or less successfully, be expressed in propositions that are presented for our belief, but that belief is not the equivalent of faith. It is only one expression of faith.

Seventh, for Scholastics, faith controlled freedom as the banks of a river controlled its flow. That is, its control came from outside – it was extrinsic. For Lynch, freedom may be viewed as the very stuff of faith. Once a person accepts the self, with its finite limits, as the "other" of God, as a grace, one aspires to a dependent autonomy. That is how one is to fit into reality. Perhaps the difference is contained in the fact that when Scholastics considered faith, they focused on the banks within which the river flows, whereas Lynch saw faith as the flowing, life-giving water itself. Freedom is intrinsic to faith, not extrinsic.

Finally, for Scholastics, faith is untouched by history. True, it did come *in* history, but it was unconditioned *by* history. Faith was viewed by the Scholastics as univocal. It meant the same thing for everyone, everywhere, at all times. The same truth that fell from heaven in ancient days is to be preserved undefiled as the one deposit of faith. For Lynch, faith is analogical. It is brand-new each time it is posited. Faith is historical, and very much conditioned by history. Salvation for the rich will look very different from salvation for the poor. Of course there are dogmas that need to be preserved, but not as univocal bits of information that are to remain uncontaminated by history. Faith, for Lynch, should always smell of life.

These several shifts from the Scholastic paradigm of faith do not signal a departure, but they do constitute a call to a way of thinking that more appropriately responds to life and faith as we experience it today. Scholasticism was a new step that was taken in theology during the last part of the nineteenth century, and it led to the discovery of the true impact of Thomistic thought, especially as it was recovered by Rousselot and Maréchal. Lynch's thought should be seen in furtherance of that Scholastic effort to bring Thomas's theology more fully to bear on the unique problems of our day. Our debt to Scholastics is large, but it is most appropriately paid by the advances made by one like William Lynch.

IV. The Contributions of William Lynch

A. Theological Contributions

As a contributor to the modern paradigm, Lynch has participated in the general movement that sought to correct the deficiencies of Scholasticism. But Lynch's theological insights were significant even within the modern paradigm. His contributions may be considered in four areas: faith as imagination; faith as drama; faith as the perfection of freedom; and faith as the reconciliation of contraries.

i. Faith as Imagination. One of Lynch's main contributions to theology is his treatment of faith as imagination. Rousselot had already drawn on Thomas' thought in proposing the primacy of the intuition as that which brings a person in touch with the real. Rousselot even recognized the value of art and history in their ability to pose the particular in apprehensions that, "are 'more real' though less easily fixed, and which are more complete even though in themselves . . . less certain." Although human intuition is not perfect, its value needs to be recognized, since the Scholastic alternative, the reduction of all reality to the rational, denies both chance and freedom, two elements of reality that have come to play prominent roles in modern thought.[18]

That fundamental rediscovery of the role of the intuition constituted an enormous step forward in Catholic theology. Theologians like Cirne-Lima have since then developed theologies that have built on that insight and have thereby granted an important place to lived experience, and whatever can bring that

---

18. Rousselot, *The Intellectualism of St. Thomas*, 111, 113. It is interesting that Rousselot used the life of the imagination in the way Lynch would propose years later. For example, he refers to the experiences of a character in a novel, John Henry Newman's *Loss and Gain*, to explore a point on faith in "Les Yeux de la foi," 252.

experience to concrete expression. Lynch's concept of the imagination parallels and extends the notion of the intuition that those
theologians have developed. Lynch's thoughts reflect Cirne-
Lima's proposal that the intuition produces images for the mind's
eye to look into. Those images constitute self-disclosures of
reality. They give evidence for the real, and they form the source
of concepts, judgments, and syllogisms, and, we might add with
Lynch, whether we realize it or not, those images are packed with
both choices and affections one way or another.[19]

Lynch maintained that faith at its core is not a separate
experience, but the way we experience. As Lynch proposed, faith
is a way of producing images and a way of assembling the facts
so they become intelligible as evidence that the world is more
like the one portrayed by images of faith than not.

In addition, Lynch would agree that faith is related to
intuition in its broader, more popular sense. Intuition here means
the process that enables a person to assess a given situation
quickly without the formal labors of discursive analysis.[20] Intuition in this sense is the result of a rapid judgment about a concrete
situation on the basis of talent and experience. For example, the
chess master can look at a complex arrangement of pieces at
midgame, and within a few seconds, propose the strongest
possible move. Or the expert mechanic can listen to the weaken-
ing pulse of an engine and go right to the source of the difficulty.
Psychologist Herbert Simon contends that there is nothing mystical about this type of intuition. After enough study and practice
in a given area, a talented person who enjoys that type of work

---

19. One complaint of modern philosophers is that philosophy had too long been
carried on with visual metaphors for knowing. Perhaps the fault is that only
one of the five senses was used. A more analogical approach, using all five
senses, and integrating insights from the various arts and sciences might have
yielded more satisfactory results.

20. Intuition in this sense is different from the technical way the term was used
by Cirne-Lima. Here it is closely related to Newman's concept of natural
inference (the illative sense) by which people reason not from propositions
to propositions, but "from concrete to concrete, from wholes to wholes." This
trait enables the peasant to predict the weather with some confidence, and
the experienced physician to give quick and accurate diagnoses. It is the
suitable handling of facts. See *Grammar of Assent,* supra at 260-62, 267. In
Lynch's terms, it would be similar to the sensibility of faith.

naturally builds an intuitive sense for the dynamics that are involved in quickly solving problems in that area. The grand master's eyes will light up as he perceives certain clusters of pieces arranged just so on the board. He knows from experience the range of possibilities that can result from such clusters. He has an intuition of what to do with those pieces. That intuition is analogous to the sensibility of faith in the personal context. It allows the faithful person to respond to a given situation appropriately without the studied effort of a novice. Simon describes intuition as

> the ability to recognize a friend and to receive and to retrieve from memory all the things you've learned about the friend in the years that you've known him. And of course if you know a lot about the friend, you'll be able to make good judgments about him.[21]

The ability to recognize the friend is analogous to the central core of faith. The ability to respond appropriately to the friend is analogous to the sensibility of faith. The good judgments about the friend are analogous to beliefs that come from faith.

Of course, the problem in religious faith comes with the difficulty in testing the intuition. The intuition of the master chess player or master mechanic is easily tested. The game is won or it is not. The engine idles smoothly or it falters. In the area of faith, if we "intuit" the possibility that God, our "easily recognized friend," allows a life of indifference to the poor, then how are we to answer? If the person claims to be a Christian, then citation of various biblical passages will have to be explained credibly (e.g., Mt. 25). In addition, veneration of saints who spent their lives in service to the poor would also require suitable explanation. If the person disclaims the Christian God, then the discussion may focus on the value of compassion in life. Does love for the poor produce a more dignified human being, or does it produce merely impoverishment? At this point, believer and nonbeliever alike hunt for "evidence," or facts, or experiences that will make their own position unassailable or "evident." They will scan the expanse of

---

21. Simon, *Reason in Human Affairs* (Stanford: Stanford University Press, 1983), 27.

human experience in search of images that will show us whether compassion is to be encouraged.

Here, Lynch's contributions come to the fore. The arts form a large part of that evidence for faith which, as imagination, contains both a reproductive and a productive aspect. That is, the arts might even produce what we are looking for. Composer Aaron Copland claimed that

> a master work awakens in us reactions of a spiritual order that are already in us, only waiting to be aroused. When Beethoven's music exhorts us to 'be noble,' 'be compassionate,' 'be strong,' he awakens moral ideas that are already within us. His music cannot persuade: it makes evident. It does not shape conduct: it is itself the exemplification of a particular way of looking at life. A concert is not a sermon. It is a performance – a reincarnation of a series of ideas implicit in the work of art.[22]

Of course, this does not mean that nobility, for example, is not really in the soul or that it is only a wish or a projection. But it does mean that it is not always easily recognized. It needs to be made evident. It needs to become tangible in some way. Then others may see for themselves whether analogous qualities, though unseen, may be detected within their own lives too. In similar fashion we yearn to make the presence of God evident through our lives. We seek to make that presence tangible, so much so that it might become part of what Vatican I called the "great and perpetual motive of credibility" that is the Church (DS 3013). Then the "exterior facts" of the Church can meet the "interior facts" of a person's life, and that person may grow in faith together with the Church.

Faith is the imagination which produces images that become evidence for living life according to that faith. Fullness of life in its deepest meaning should be the result of faith. If we rely on an offhand "intuition" in the broad sense, it may mislead us into an impossible position. The endgame may be imminent. That is one reason the Christian faithful are careful to maintain a memory of their saints. Christianity's saints are those whose

---

22. Copland, *Music and Imagination*, 16-17.

experience and love in leading faithful lives make them intuitive grand masters. They could size up a situation and tell us what the loving response requires. Just as novice chess players study the grand masters to gain a feel for creating advantageous positions on the chess board, so too Christians study the lives of saints. Hence, the lives of saints like Mother Frances Cabrini should be consulted for an authentic intuitive sense of what the Christian faith involves.[23] Not all intuitive perceptions are equal. It is often the task of theology to construct methods and criteria for sorting out reliable intuitions from mere projections or illusions. Theology at its most basic level offers a critique of the imagination. It seeks to build a reliable pitch pipe that will enable us to handle God's word at the right pitch.

Granted that the images present in the arts, history, drama, etc., are important bearers of experience, how can theology actually learn from them? What principles will reliably guide theologians in their efforts to glean the truth from those images? Those are the questions that Lynch answers, and that is his place in the theological effort. His theology offers a penetrating critique of images and the imagination that produces them. Lynch counsels the theologian that faithfulness to the divine cannot be achieved apart from faithfulness to the concrete reality we encounter everyday. Recall Lynch's image of the fish: "it must breathe its air (the infinite) through the water (the finite); if it should pursue its goal more directly, the process of abandoning the water to get the air would end in agony and death."[24] Lynch's

---

23. We might note that chessboards have not changed throughout the centuries, but the terrain on which Christian life is played varies substantially from age to age. It follows that Christians look for moves that are analogous, not identical, to the moves of their ancestors in faith. We should also recall here George Tyrrell's caution that we ought to pay more attention to the conclusions of the saints than to their rational analyses of situations. *Nova et Vetera*, 169. However, we must exercise some discretion even in accepting the moral intuitions of saints, an observation stemming from a perusal of the correspondence between St. Augustine and St. Jerome, who were not above attacking each other in quite vivid terms.

24. *CA* 76. An example of how Lynch would advise us to remain faithful to concrete, finite reality is found in his treatment of time. "[T]here is an amazing refusal on the part of modern 'sensibility and experience' to discuss, much less take as an example, the non-miraculous quality in Christ's resolute living

doctrines of emergence and diffraction make the arts primary contributors in the theological effort. His observations concerning the absolutizing instinct, the Promethean imagination, and the importance of keeping contraries together also offer valuable guidance to the theologian.

One might consider Lynch's contribution in terms of Lonergan's four levels of consciousness and intentionality. Part of the shift to the modern paradigm included a shift away from Scholastic "faculty psychology," which offered a formal, analytical, separate discussion of each of the personal faculties. Scholars moved toward an interest in "intentionality analysis" that considered how those powers were put to use in the concrete. Lonergan distinguished four different levels of consciousness and intentionality: the empirical, the intellectual, the rational, and the responsible. At the *empirical* level, a person senses, perceives, imagines, feels, speaks, and moves. At the *intellectual* level, the person understands something, expresses that understanding, and attempts to deal with presuppositions and implications. At the *rational* level, the person reflects, gathers evidence, and judges whether the understanding has expressed a true or false proposition. Finally, at the *responsible* level, the person decides what goals to set and how to attain those goals. Each level is sublated by the next. Each assumes the preceding level and then exceeds it by attaining a new level of consciousness and intentionality.

Lynch's contribution consists in his discussion of the impact of that first transcendental level at which the person is asked to be attentive. The images that a person perceives can carry a profound impact in a person's life. People not only perceive, but they perceive according to a pattern, a paradigm. They perceive according to an imagination or according to a faith. When the object of their perception is life itself as it is lived in the presence of the divine, then images of faith come to the fore.

Attentiveness to human experience calls for an appropriation of the images that artists render as a result of their experience of

---

and penetration into human time." *CA* 53. He succinctly stated his position in commenting on good literary criticism: "Let there be no nontemporal short cuts to the truth." *CA* 64 n. 19.

life. Furthermore, given Lynch's insight that images think and feel, he shows how images carry forward the "attentive" stage into the intellectual stage of understanding by virtue of their capacity to display otherwise hidden facets of their being. A worthy image carries with it its own presuppositions and implications that it will reveal to those who know how to handle images skillfully. Good images display heuristic qualities that enable us to understand more about the object of the image. In addition, the impact of the image is felt at the rational level by virtue of its ability to relate itself to what is understood in other images. New evidence for the truth of the image will arise from its interplay with other images, concepts, judgments, and decisions. Images think. They carry their own rationality with them. As a person is faithful to an image, new doors will open to other areas not seen initially. Finally, Lynch has shown that images carry with them an entire history of predilections and choices that have already been made. As a commitment to an image is made, a whole series of decisions is implied. It follows that the impact of the imagination is felt even at the level of responsibility. Hence, all four levels of consciousness and intentionality. are intrinsically, not merely extrinsically, affected by the images we choose. That intrinsic relationship would also hold for the relationship between faith's images and attentiveness, understanding, rationality, and responsibility.[25]

---

25. An example of the image's effect throughout the four transcendental levels may be found in the work of Aeschylus. He offered a new image of justice through his *Oresteia,* which led to an understanding of the equitable demands of justice. It also enabled people to advance in the rational use of the principles of justice as they relate to other principles and sensibilities. Faithfulness to his images of justice also commit a person to more responsible decisions. For a treatment of Lynch's contribution in terms of Karl Rahner's transcendental Thomism, see William V. Dych, "Moving on to Fresh Horizons: The Discoveries of Karl Rahner and William Lynch," *The Catholic Mind* (September 1978): 189-205. Father Dych offers the example of the old dogma, *extra ecclesiam, nulla salus* [outside the church, there is no salvation]. Such a dogma made sense when practically everyone in the known European world was a member of the Church. As Christian awareness of the world outside Europe grew, the dogma made less sense. Instead of searching for new images of salvation, theologians tended to engage in intellectual gymnastics to salvage the dogma through speculations about limbo, the baptism of desire, and the like. Dych, "Fresh Horizons," 9-10. It appears that the Church could use a Christian Aeschylus to move it beyond some of its dogmatic ruts on the road to salvation.

As noted above, each transcendental level is sublated by the next. It includes the previous level and also exceeds it. Lynch's insights indicate that the level is not an "adding onto" but an unfolding. The "higher viewpoint" is not attained by leaving the object's image to go to a plane once removed from the object. It is a plunging into the object. Perhaps it is better to speak not of a "higher" viewpoint, but of a "deeper" viewpoint. One attains that viewpoint not by leaving the object for someplace "higher," but by entering more deeply into it. That entrance occurs through our poetic ability to describe, or redescribe, things through the images that we apply to them and derive from them. Lynch offers us guidance as we attempt this undertaking through the arts.

Insofar as theology trusts and returns to its normative images, it is at its bedrock. It can come no closer to human experience than its images. The rest is ineffable. Faith generates and applies Christian images to life, and thus informs life according to a Christian imagination. Lynch gives us a way to care for those images, distinguish them, keep them alive, and so keep our faith in God alive. If concepts are to be driven back into our experiences to purify them, then they must be driven back into the images through which our experiences are mediated. Thus a work like Paul Ricoeur's *Symbolism of Evil* represents theology at its most basic level. Lynch pushes theology into the world of the image maker so that theologians may learn from those images. Lynch's theology assumes that we do not automatically know who God is, but must work hard for fruitful images that are at once concrete and revelatory of the divine. He constantly criticizes those artists who seem to be fashioning images only out of concepts, and he repeatedly returns to those whose images spring from the experience of life itself.

Faith is not merely "a conceptual bundle of ideas which must beg imaginative support from literature and art." Of course, it includes that "bundle of ideas," but never apart from the intuitions – the images – that faith produces. Faith is not the child of Apollo. Lynch here agrees with Nietzsche in rejecting the life of an Apollo whose guiding light comes merely from the top of his head. Lynch uses the figure of Apollo to criticize those who allow themselves, in their visions of faith, to soar into a sort of infinite dream, to bypass the concrete stuff of this world in an attempt to reach a purely ecstatic position where they can grasp truth as it is in the act of falling from heaven. Lynch parts company with Nietzsche in his choice of gods. Nietzsche chooses Dionysus, the god of revelry. If Apollo's virtues spun from his head, imposing ethereal limits on the human, Dionysus' virtue escapes all limits. Dionysus is given to ecstatic revelry that totally escapes the rational.[26]

Lynch chooses Jesus Christ as the one who encapsulates the infinite depths of the divine by remaining faithful to the very definite, concrete contours of his existence. Jesus is the perfect revelation of God, yet he is the one who could say, "I thirst." Truly Christian concepts do not come by way of deductive reasoning unless the premise is firmly rooted in the concrete and the definite dimensions of this world. This world in its concrete fullness *is* the truth that has fallen from heaven. The problem is how to be faithful to it, loving it as "God's other" and thereby learning its secrets.

ii. Faith as Drama. Lynch's work might also be seen as an extension of Blondel's theology of action. Blondel proposed that action can contain what thought can only approximate. Faith consists of that action by which two lives unite. It is not simply the thought about those lives. Faith's action also involves a submission to what God has revealed to us.

Lynch would accept those notions while casting them in somewhat different terms. Lynch urged that life consists not only of the *drama* of action but also of the *pathos* of submission to that which is not subject to our control. If the clash of *drama* and *pathos* is negotiated successfully by our faithfulness to the concrete through which the divine is found, then *mathos*, a stage of new insight, will be bestowed upon us.[27] Lynch then suggests the arts, especially drama, as a worthy heuristic device to unfold the implications of our actions and of Christ's actions outside the

---

26. *CA* vii, xii. Lynch, "Euripides' 'Bacchae': The Mind in Prison," *Cross Currents* 25 (summer 1975): 170-72.

27. See chap. Three, pp. 93-95, above, for a discussion of this movement of *drama*, *pathos*, and *mathos*.

theater. The arts are part of the creative, active paradigm of faith.[28]
The light of faith constantly changes to catch our recognition of
the unchanging constancy of God's love. Action thus characterizes
both faith and its light.

As Blondel proposed a method of immanence, so Lynch
proposed a method steeped in the concrete nature of this world
as God's other. The dynamism that fueled Blondel's method of
immanence was the disproportion of the "willing will," which
forever reaches for the infinite, and of the "willed will," which
posits actual choices that never satisfy the willing will. That same
dynamism is posited by Lynch in the metaphysics of interpenetration. The deepest dimension of the finite is found in its ability
to communicate the infinite.

The disproportion of the will analyzed by Blondel is seen
analogously at all levels of being through Lynch's analysis of the
one and the many. The will is only one instance of the dynamic
interplay between God as "One," and creation as God's "Other."
That same dynamism reaches throughout our being. Just as the
will is a reflection of that relationship that cannot be satisfied by
individual finite choices, so too our intellects, our emotions, our

28. In "Liturgy and Theatre," *Liturgical Arts* 12 (November 1943): 3-10, Lynch traces
the historical rise of the modern theatre in the West. Its beginnings are not
found to derive from the ancient Greek or Latin theatres, but from medieval
liturgical theatre where dramas were placed in the context of worship. "The
liturgy was increasingly dramatic and its symbolism was but a step removed
from formal drama. . . . The Church was theologically convinced that its whole
inner life was a sort of drama, whose province was the reproduction on a
social scale of the life of its Founder." Ibid., 3. Thus, the Church building could
stand for the lower reaches of hell in ceremonies that depict Christ's descent
into hell. This symbolism was also met with an un-Platonic realism that equated
truth with the historical Christ. Thus Passion plays related every realistic detail
they could in their attempt to attend to the "passion of God." Those who
defended the use of images against the iconoclasts insisted "on the doctrinal
necessity of the human figure of Christ, the Virgin and the saints . . . the second
council of Nicaea in 787 pronounced anathema 'On him who does not admit
an explanation of the Gospel through images.'" Ibid., 4. These liturgical dramas
frequently invited the audience to cross the line from being mere spectators
to being worshipers just as "liturgical personages, whether chorus or cantor
or presiding bishop of the day's ceremonies, merged readily with the drama
– not to mention the reverse." Ibid., 9. These plays constituted an early attempt
by the Church to experiment with drama as a heuristic device to bring the
implications of the faith to bear on the contemporary setting.

relationships, and even our quest to be our "ownmost" selves cannot be satisfied without a complete bestowal of the "One" upon whom we depend. After all, it is only by virtue of the One that the many have their identity, their deepest relationship with others, and, therefore, the fulfillment of their capabilities.

iii. Faith and Freedom. Lynch's project is also in furtherance of the phenomenological-existentialist exploration of freedom as among the most splendid of human faculties. Lynch attempts to develop a theology that grants people the dignity of human autonomy and that at the same time derives its dignity from the recognition of the source of that autonomy, the sovereignty of God. Human autonomy and divine sovereignty are contraries that vary in direct proportion. Lynch's theology thus may be seen as an extension of the concerns of Karl Rahner, Gabriel Marcel, Paul Ricoeur, and others. Lynch would again offer the arts as a worthy vehicle of exploration into freedom, and as one of the means by which that freedom is realized.

Lynch thus would be critical of the conception of law and power that formed the basis of certain Scholastic documents, particularly during the Modernist controversy. The relationship between truth and authority is not as simple as some would propose. Premature bridling of human freedom based on old Scholastic a priori arguments have led to various traps from which there appeared to be no graceful escape. For example, Scholasticism led some to the contention that slavery is allowable under natural law, and, consequently, is an acceptable practice for the faithful. The Scholastic inability to relativize belief in the Pauline epistles concerning slavery accounted for that strange position. As such, it represented an enormous failure in the use of theological concepts that have been cut loose from their intuitive moorings. It also offered a telling commentary on the relative value of freedom in the Scholastic paradigm. Slavish adherence to doctrines led to other questionable contentions such as Camillo Mazzella's assertion that God created the heavens and earth in six ordinary days, complete with fossils ("in statu perfecto"). His thought constituted not so much a rational hypothesis explaining the facts as the upholding of the univocal requirements of

Scholastic belief. So too with Pius XII's misgivings concerning polygenism (*Humani Generis*, AAS 576).[29]

When faith can be used to justify slavery, to argue that God created fossils as we find them today, and to recommend monogenism, then faith itself has become a trap. The *drama* of such faith inevitably produces a *pathos*, a suffering, that calls for a "descent into hell." A painful dispossession of some of the rock-hard certainties of Scholasticism then needs to be endured. But it takes real freedom to become unstuck. The path taken in one of Lynch's most challenging books, *Christ and Prometheus*, accomplishes some of this purifying descent.[30] Human autonomy must be taken seriously. It must be listened to and reverenced as a grace from the divine.

Lynch's thoughts on the relationship of faith and time have proven to be particularly productive in this area. It is in virtue of time that freedom exists. The very structure of time parallels the structure of faith. Time's irony is needed as a vehicle for a faith that proposes that what dies also rises, just as each moment of time dies only to give rise a to new moment. Furthermore, Lynch's penetrating analysis of the stages of faith constitutes an original contribution to the theology of faith. Although von Hügel had already proposed stages of faith that parallel the imaginative, the

---

29. It is interesting that some Scholastic theologians had sense enough not to pay attention to their own method when it came to issues of slavery. Those theologians condemned slavery, made liberal use of history to relativize the Church's position, and paid mere lip service to what was supposedly permitted under the natural law. For a brief example of this methodological sleight of hand, see James J. Fox, "Slavery, Ethical Aspect of," in *Catholic Encyclopedia*, vol. 14, ed. C. G. Herbermann et al. (New York: Robert Appleton, 1912): 39–41. Talar, *Metaphor and Modernist*, 101.

30. There Lynch cautioned us that the fact that a finite object could be considered as having an ultimate meaning does not imply that it cannot have a meaning of its own. Too often our view of the ultimate purpose of things obfuscates the little purpose, the little meaning of things. In that little purpose and meaning resides great value. We must listen to it and reverence it before we assume a supposedly divine point of view. Lynch is suggesting that perhaps the little meaning of things, the meaning that we can understand readily, ironically contains the ultimate meaning. Perhaps the little *is* the big. That is the irony of faith. It is only by listening to God's other, creation, that we learn about God. We learn nothing by imposing our preconceived notion of God onto the little beings of creation.

intellectual, and the intuitive levels of cognition, Lynch's seven stages convey the taste of the struggle of life itself. The stages of faith describe not only a movement through time, but even more so, a movement toward consciously embraced freedom. The life of faith seems to evolve with the expectations, disappointments, hopes, and insights in the way Lynch presented them. His unflinching look at death and his confidence in the irony of faith need to be considered by all who are fashioning their faith.

Time makes freedom possible, and freedom is of the essence of faith. If faith is personal knowledge, not merely a bundle of concepts, then people must be free to commit themselves to God through a personal commitment to Jesus with one another in the Holy Spirit. Modern experience has told us that the identity of a person is not a pregiven fact that is to be reported. It is the human project to freely fashion a self by the way one gives the self. We do not first fashion a self and then give it away. The giving is the fashioning. The losing is the finding. As people report the results of their projects through their images of the noble human being as well as images of failed attempts, faith collaborates with the arts, and it is enriched in the process.

iv. Faith in the Midst of Contraries. The subjectively inspired heart and objectively rational head must inform each other. Lynch claimed that there is a unity of sensibility that keeps them together.[31] To attempt to cut one off from the other is like attempting to cut a log in such a way that there will no more left side of the log. The attempt is the result of an illusion that sets a person up to make the mistakes of either the hard-hearted rationalist or the irrational dreamer. Both head and heart involve a single sensibility. That is to say, faith is analogical. Many aspects need to be held in the correct proportion to each other – contraries included.

The richness and complexity of life's images instilled in Lynch a profound distrust of those who deal facilely in terms of intellectual absolutes. The presence of the divine is a subtle presence, and the absolutizing instinct can ring so loudly that it

---

31. *IM* 131, 136, 143.

effectively overwhelms the divine presence and instills a sensibility that is foreign to the Christian spirit. Lynch does not deny the absolute. He illustrates its subtlety. The absolute is found in the way a life is lived, not in the concepts that attempt to define it. We discuss the absolute, but only in relative terms. It is part of faith's irony to convey the lofty absolute through the lowly relative, and to convey the sense of the faith through the rationality of its images of love.

The certitude of the Christian faith then expresses itself not in the external objectivity of a syllogism whose major and minor premises result from personages who lived thousands of years ago. The certitude of faith for Lynch becomes lodged right in the experience of life itself because it is through faith's images that the person lives. Faith then is transformed into the confidence of living the rich, fruitful life that was commended to us by Jesus: a life of imagination characterized by faith, hope, and love.

There is also a unity of sensibility by which the knower and the known, the subject and the object, are known only in relation to each other.[32] We never come to know the object without also coming to some self-awareness as well. Given the unity of experience through images, that is, given the image's ability to contain not only the mutual presence of two people but also its ability to contain their meaning to one another in the poetic dimension, we can see how Lynch, contrary to Scholastic tradition, avoids a dualistic conception that attempts to place a person in two different worlds at once, each with its own sensibility. Lynch proposed that those "two" worlds are really one. People should not compare their experience of the world to their experience of faith. Faith is a way of experiencing the grace in this world while coming to some awareness of one's God and one's self in the process.[33]

---

32. *IM* 131, 136, 143.

33. If the world of faith and the modern world were two different entities, the dehumanizing effects of this world would never touch the faithful. But they do. The faithful see the dehumanizing effects of the modern barrage of meaningless data, advertising images, and pornographic entertainment, and therefore, see its de-divinizing effects as well. William F. Lynch, *Image Industries* (New York: Sheed and Ward, 1959).

Some may hesitate to consider faith as imagination because one might become so lost in the subjective dimension that the very notion of objective dogma may be jeopardized. Lynch was quite definite in his defense of dogma. For example, Lynch insisted that Christians can place no hope in images of self-absorption. The life, passion, death, and resurrection of Jesus furnish the norm here. There is no turning back from the cross. Philosophical and theological expressions of that truth will help the community to apply that image, but they can never change it. The Pelagian attempt to exclude God from the work of salvation is a vain attempt to exclude the divine from the human, just as the Gnostic attempt to achieve divine insight apart from the concrete world is a vain attempt to exclude the human from the divine.

Lynch was eager to preserve the objective pole of faith. The objective norm that is followed in matters of faith consists of the concrete images founded on Jesus' life, which furnishes the foundation for our lives as Christians. Obviously disputes will arise, but the debate must include reference to the norm that all attempt to follow. Valid interpretations of texts need to be attained using the guidelines suggested by Lynch and by others who are sensitive to the complexities of the poetic and interpersonal dimensions of the Scriptures. But rules of interpretation alone can do only so much for us. It takes a faithful person to recognize the norm properly, and to use it as the risen Jesus would to guide his flock. That is, Tradition, the faith as lived authentically, is an important component of that norm. Both good decisions and bad decisions have been made, and will continue to be made, as long as we live on this side of the Second Coming. But our effort is carried on primarily in terms of the concrete images of Scripture and the experience of mature witnesses who attempt to pattern life after those images. This should be a self-correcting endeavor that welcomes every voice that honestly reports an experience of Christian living. Both bishops and prophets need to be heard. Both have erred in the past, but both have also saved the Church.

Lynch would insist that faith is not relative in the sense that it can mean anything at all, but it is relational in the sense that it always is related to a concrete historical people. Faith must be related to a particular history and culture, or it will have nothing to do with real people. Keeping faith relational prevents us from fashioning idols and enables us to perceive indirectly the absolute love that sent Jesus to the cross.[34]

Of course, to treat faith as imagination is not to give free reign to a person's ability to construct fantasy. Lynch insists that the function of the imagination is to imagine the real. But the real is not univocal. This imagination of the real is accomplished by trusting the images we know best of all (the concrete, the finite) before we begin to posit images of God. Fantastic images give rise only to false hopes and frustrations. If my "faith" allows me to imagine a clear path where there is only a brick wall, obviously there will not be much progress. Faith comes from the outside. It comes from hearing the testimony of others. But once that testimony is heard, the imagination of faith must structure an anological inner world that corresponds to the outer world in meaningful ways, or else it must remain largely without effect. There are productive ways to do this, as well as unproductive ways. The difference is known through its fruitfulness or its adequacy in guiding us in the drama of human life.[35]

Once faith is considered as imagination, the Christian can see how faith can affect virtually every aspect of life. Faith is the ultimate context because it is open to mystery. Faith should be

---

34. While dogmatic decisions are necessary, philosophical or theological expressions cannot claim the same level of truth as the concrete images of Jesus' life. Dogmatic concepts are epistemologically secondary to the concrete images, or intuitions, from which they are derived. That holds true even for the more "theological" sections of Scripture as opposed to its narrative sections. Paul's theology of the cross is profound, but it is not to be considered on the same level as the cross itself or the Passion narratives.

35. For example, scientific paradigms are useful for a whole range of activities, including nuclear physics. However, the nuclear paradigm has its limits. Consider, for example, a cake recipe expressed in terms of the molecules and atomic particles that make up the cake. It might be accurate in one sense, but Betty Crocker's way of writing recipes seems to be more promising for the purposes of baking an appetizing cake. Faith proposes images for living in relation to a person's total context, which will be more adequate and fruitful than other images a person might use. See Garrett Green, *Imaging God: Theology and the Religious Imagination* (New York: Harper and Row, 1989), 59. Although Green does not cite Lynch's work, his conception of faith as the "paradigmatic imagination" parallels Lynch's concept of faith as imagination. Ibid., 66-70, 134, 144.

at home with all other fruitful paradigms and contexts in a culture. Faith as imagination unifies not only the outside world but also the inside world. Head and heart no longer need to be at odds with each other, but as mutually illuminating when it comes to personal knowledge. Faith, of course, will not add directly to our knowledge of physics or chemistry, but neither will it detract. Faith adds the poetic dimension, the dimension of meaning. It is a domain in which rationality plays a role along with commitment. Faith as imagination highlights the elements of faith that make it intrinsic to the believer's life, without which faith would appear only as a collection of foreign curiosities.

B. What Difference Does It Make?

If we adopt Lynch's notions of faith as imagination, there ought to be some discernible benefit for our life of faith. In other words, what difference would it make if we were to accept Lynch's thoughts on faith? Certainly many who followed Scholasiticism maintained a profound faith in the deepest sense of the word. Many of them became saints because of their religion, not in spite of it. What is at issue is an appropriate way to conceptualize that faith, not the quality of faith of those who held various theories.

Aside from the fact that imagination has always been a part of faith and is necessary in order for us to account for it in cognitional theory, we might turn to the more practical setting for an answer. For example, if faith were only belief, then the docile plea, "Father, tell me what I have to believe," would make some sense. Faith in that context is a matter of additional information that might be elicited to fill in the gaps in our knowledge. It is a faith in which we have all the answers. Such faith presumably could fit into any imaginative framework. Thus we might believe various truths but fail to integrate them into the larger context of life, which might well be carried on in terms of an altogether different paradigm (life as the jungle or as the marketplace, etc.). The admonition to such a faith was usually the ineffective indictment: "But you don't really believe!" The imagination does not contest how "hard" we believe, but it seeks to integrate our lives in such a way that those beliefs make some sense in terms of the larger background of our lives.

Faith is impossible without imagination. "Father, tell it to me straight," is the request of a starved, impoverished imagination, an attempt at univocity where there can only be analogy, poetic meaning, and the deeper significations of mystery. Such an attempt at univocal faith might tell us that there are obstacles on a path, but it will not inform us of their significance. It might offer the Ten Commandments as a guide, but, unaided, it will not produce a metanoia, or a change of mind, that enables us to accept the irony of existence. It will sing the psalm, but not at the right pitch. It will offer religion, but its use will remain unclear. Then faith can be used as a retreat from life, an opiate, rather than the very terms in which life can be lived.

Faith as imagination offers a synthesis, a whole, in terms of which we can proceed with interpersonal relationships and situate ourselves vis-à-vis the divine. It is not merely a collection of beliefs, it is an environment. Therefore, it is relevant to every facet of life, not merely the intellectual facet. Infants can be baptized into the faith precisely because faith can be seen as imagination. Beliefs are the results of judgments that infants are incapable of making. But any infant is committed to an environment in spite of itself. With baptism, responsible adults assure us that the infant's imagination, its environment, its "primal faith," is the start of a Christian faith. Appropriate beliefs, as well as an education of mind and heart, should follow in due course. Later, the Church sacramentally confirms that such is the case.

Faith should reflect the revelation of God. Christians are confident that their faith in Jesus Christ (i.e., their acceptance of his images of reality as historically realized in his person) opens doors to the deepest interpersonal levels of truths that disclose, and that even create by the grace of God, experiences of God. The disclosure/creation of the experience of God is not a fantasy. Even an ordinary friendship is constituted not only by disclosures but also by the creation of a relationship. New power is found in that relationship because it consists of more than merely the information that one person discloses once and for all to the other. It also consists of the new creation of mutual appreciation. A new sensibility is brought to the fore. Once we bring a new attitude to life as a result of our faith, we can say that the new attitude is "created" but not "made up," and that the attitude is revelatory of the divine.

A concrete example of a typical act of faith may help to clarify the issues. The Christian believes that Jesus is living, and is exalted at the right hand of the Father. Therefore, it makes sense to "talk" to Jesus in prayer. As it is, I imagine Jesus if only as a dialogue partner when I pray. I am not praying to a figment of my imagination, yet the situation is much more subtle than is usually conceived. Those without my faith would say I am speaking only to myself. Insofar as a human being is already a word spoken by God, Karl Rahner conceived of prayer as a sort of interior dialogue with the self, but not to the exclusion of God.[36] The dialogue includes God, not as a "speaker" in the simplistic sense, nor as the prayer's "listener" in the simplistic sense, but as the one who enables the "dialogue" to take place and to take place in the way that it does. In other words, God affects both the very awareness of the person as well as the imagination of the person because the images in which the person prays are fundamentally formed by the person's familiarity with God's self-disclosure in Scripture. The way in which those images are used is given to the person through Tradition or through the practice of the faith in the community enlivened by the Holy Spirit. By virtue of the person's connection with the Tradition, there is a concrete connection with the Holy Spirit who has been present to that person and to that Tradition in the body of sensibility of the faith. The prayer of the person is not only a figment of the person's imagination. The act of imagination in faith is an ontological reaching to God. It is the Holy Spirit who prays within that person who speaks with Jesus because the dialogue is enabled by God, and it is taking place according to the ironic Christic imagination as it has been lived in the Tradi-tion.[37] In other words, my prayer can be in the Holy Spirit,

---

36. Karl Rahner, *The Practice of Faith: A Handbook of Contemporary Spirituality*, ed. K. Lehmann and A. Raffelt (New York: Crossroad, 1983), 94.

37. In a sense, the "words of Jesus" that occur to me in prayer can be considered as authentic to the extent that the faith that produces them is pure, i.e., an imagination informed by the ironic Christic imagination. But we need not claim

through Jesus, to the Father. Prayer is not less than is usually imagined, but is much more.

Any person's ongoing discourse with Jesus can take place only in the imagination. Where else can it take place? How else can we conceive of a Jesus who speaks English?[38] The imagination is the meeting place of all that I am with all that I am not. In other words, the imagination provides a sort of interior forum for prayer to Jesus. That forum is faith. In that forum, Jesus as risen "hears" my prayer since it is his Spirit that in effect has informed that prayer through the ironic Christic imagination. The interior dialogue is both with myself and with Jesus. In prayer, we ought not attempt to divide artificially what is "from" the person as opposed to what is "from" Jesus. Prayer is found in the unification of the person and the divine, not in their separation.[39]

The extent to which the prayer is really with Jesus depends on the purity of faith a person brings to the dialogue. In other words, a robber's prayer for a successful heist is not a prayer in dialogue with Jesus. It is not informed with the supernatural faith that is needed for real prayer.[40] Furthermore, as faith's images unfold their implications for my particular situation, an "answer" may occur to me that can be considered as being "from Jesus" in the sense that it will be consistent with the faith of Jesus of Nazareth. According to the purity of the prayer, that response

---

that those words are the very words of Jesus directed to me. We might consider the analogous situation of Jesus' words at the Last Supper as those words appear in the Synoptics and in Paul. None of the quotations are identical. Moreover, the words used at the consecration at Mass are different from each of the Scriptural accounts. The important element in each account is not the "ipsissima verba Jesu," but the ecclesial faith from which those words arise. The one in personal prayer is similarly situated.

38. Karl Rahner maintained that the visions of the mystics could be presumed to be imaginative visions. Indeed, the mystical doctors, Rahner asserts, claim that imaginative visions should be regarded as more valuable and exalted than "corporeal" visions. Karl Rahner, *Visions and Prophecies* (New York: Herder and Herder, 1963), 32, 38. It might help here to recall the central role of the imagination when *any* two people communicate. Lynch held that we can get no closer to another person than through our images.

39. Karl Rahner, *Visions and Prophecies*, 63-64.

40. Garrett Green insists on the need for a "faithful imagination" that hearkens to the images proposed in Scripture. Id., *Imagining God*, 125, 134.

might be the most faithful response to God that I can make in those circumstances, and the most authentic response from God to me. As prayer takes on a communal dimension, its chances of being purified are enhanced. Who could imagine a community prayer that requests the successful completion of a sinful project?

Is the divine really aware of my prayer? Of course. The divine made the prayer possible in the first place. Can the divine intervene with an "answer" of its own? Yes, of course, but its answer need not be considered as an intervention. Since God is closer to us than we are to ourselves, the answer may come by way of "emergence." That is, an answer may occur to us by virtue of living the faith. Since one cannot come closer to another than through that person's images, it stands to reason that God's answer to prayer will come by way of the person's imagination.

Further, let us imagine that I pray for something specific, such as the health of my sick father. Then say the cure takes place. By my faith, by my imagination, I will say that my prayer has been "answered." That very way of talking requires poetic imagination because I see one thing (the health of my father) in terms of another (the answer to prayer). Now, could that "answer" have come anyway? Of course, but not as the answer to my prayer. There are many occasions of grace that go unrecognized in this world. Might the cure not have come at all but for the prayer? How can we possibly know the answer to such a question? It would be impossible to establish the point by scientific evidence. Yet the faithful do speak quite reasonably, it seems, of miraculous cures.[41] Could it be that the power of the relationship expressed

---

41. For example, John Traynor, a 40-year-old British marine, was wounded in the head in 1914. He lay unconscious for five weeks. Returning to the battlefront in 1915, he was wounded in the knee. Three months later suffered other wounds to the chest and biceps where a nerve was severed. Three attempts were made to attach the nerve ends. Amputation was recommended. Epileptic attacks complicated matters. Another attempt to connect the nerve failed. In 1920, a portion of Traynor's skull was removed. This trepanation opening measured 8" by 2". The result was partial paralysis, vertigo, and epileptic convulsions. Eventually, he lost control of his sphincters of the bladder and anus. His arm was paralyzed and muscles atrophied. This man's faith took him to Lourdes where, at the second bathing at the pool, he bled from the mouth and suffered an epileptic attack. At the ninth bathing, his legs convulsed violently. He was carried to the procession of the Blessed Sacrament, this time

in faith can be brought to bear to cure a person in such a way? If faith is imagination, there is a new creative aspect to each act of faith. Each act of faith is analogous in Lynch's terms. It is not simply "the same old song and dance" that has been going on for two thousand years. It carries with it the freshness of a newfound love. There is a real power available there. If faith is a fruitful way of imagining our relationship with God so we might place ourselves in the universe as autonomous yet dependent creatures, then, as we are in sympathetic dialogue with God, might there be an untapped power available through prayer in apt images? Might it be like striking C on the piano and hearing the sympathetic vibration of other C notes further up the scale? Might not the kingdom of God be conceived in such a way? And when the kingdom of God does arrive through a person's compassionate presence, might we not expect something of the fullness of life?

When viewed as imagination, the center of faith becomes a ground for belief. Faith as imagination offers a paradigm for the way the world operates. It constitutes a certain patterning of facts, a way of experiencing. It is the grace of interiority that perceives a certain meaning in things. Why do we believe? Among other reasons, because we have a center of faith that permits such a belief. The ultimate motive for faith is grace, the proper relation-

---

with his arms undergoing convulsions. He walked some, but collapsed. At 5:30 AM he awoke suddenly, and ran to the grotto. He recovered the full use of his right arm. The trepanation in his skull disappeared in a week. Traynor then returned to England where he sold coal, and regularly lifted 200 pound bags. He died of a hernia in 1943. See John Heaney, *The Sacred and the Psychic: Parapsychology & Christian Theology* (New York: Paulist Press, 1984), 75-6.

The cure is interesting because it took place during a time of modern critical attitudes in journalism, science, and philosophy. Those who develop theological theories need to take into account such occurrences, and deal with them in some credible way. It will not do to ignore such phenomena. Of course, their study demands a certain openness to the possibility of healing through prayer, and an awareness of the subtleties of modern theological insights. One would hope for more theological sophistication than was recently shown by researchers at four universities. Motivations for their studies included not only an interest in good health, but also the financial interests of Health Maintenance Organizations looking for a cheaper form of healing. See Joseph Pereira, "The Healing Power of Prayer Is Tested by Science," *The Wall Street Journal* (December 20, 1995), B-1, B-8.

ship between God and creation. Other reasons would include the more rational assessments of the evidence such as suggested by the so-called scientific faith of the Scholastics. Ironically, this approach would seem to include the historical-critical methods of modern exegesis. We need not apologize for having recourse to such methods. The judicious weighing of evidence is an appropriate way of forming a judgment of whether to believe or not. Such rational weighing of the evidence does not necessarily reach the center of faith unless a proposition is proposed that could not be included in faith's imaginative framework. Other reasons for believing a proposition might include psychological factors that contain a payoff of some sort to the believer. The hermeneutics of suspicion, geared toward eliciting any illegitimate payoffs, are useful in purifying ourselves of such self-serving motives for belief.

There is a group of core beliefs that are required by the Christian faith. Lynch considered historicity a crucial issue. Faith based merely on archetypes constitutes a devaluation of the actual. Lynch cautions us that the actual enactment of an archetype is never as complete, as ideal, or as real as the archetype. Furthermore, he noted that archetypes imply that the exemplars for the human lie at the beginning. Lynch believed that "a more and more human world lies ahead of us, not behind us. . . ."[42]

Historicity is crucial insofar as the Christian believes that Jesus lived his life, ministered, and died in a way that is consonant with biblical stories, and subsequently rose in a fashion that defies historical description. Within those limits, two Christians may hold different opinions about the historicity of various scriptural passages. For example, two Christians may agree on the meaning of the raising of Lazarus in terms of the life-saving significance of the kingdom of God as it is present in Jesus. They may even agree that the story anticipates the resurrection. However, a faithful person might doubt the historicity of the Lazarus passage, just as a companion in faith might believe in its historicity. Both are "faithful" followers of Christ. Both beliefs can be reasonably based

---

42. Lynch, "Archtypal Theory and Spirituality," *Studies in Formative Spirituality* 4 (February 1983): 87, 91.

on the center of faith, the paradigmatic patterning of reality as the Christian views it. The grace of faith is found more in the meaning of that particular story than on the issue of its historicity. There are some things that we simply do not know. It is not the function of supernatural faith to fill in the blanks in the historical record.[43]

When Jesus encountered the man with the withered hand and bid him to "stretch forth your hand" (Lk. 6:6-11), what is to stop us from believing that the man stretched out his hand? Must we bind ourselves to a scientific imagination that cannot fit such an event into its paradigm? Even though we do not know what happened, faith might well allow for belief in that miracle. Faith as imagination does not bind us to accept either the so-called horrendous liberal consensus that does away with the historicity of all miracles, or the so-called suffocating conservatism that insists on the simple veracity of every detail of the scriptural texts. There is a whole range of possibilities between fact and fiction, and faith as imagination is capable of tapping the riches of that range in a way that more univocally oriented approaches to faith cannot. Indeed, faith as imagination can even accommodate conflicting opinions on some significant religious issues.[44]

Does the possibility of a divergence of opinion mean that faith is arbitrary? No. Both those who believe in the historicity of a given miracle and those who do not believe offer reasons for their belief. Some reasons are better than others. Some are more convincing, others less so. Even though each can state a rationale, oftentimes neither side can offer proof that is rationally compelling. Yet each side goes through a rational process and arrives at

---

43. See Raymond Brown, *Biblical Exegesis and Church Doctrine* (New York: Paulist, 1985), 82.

44. Brown, *Biblical Exegesis and Church Doctrine*, 63-64, 82. Brown discusses the liberal and conservative extremes in chap. 3-4. For an example of the faith supporting conflicting religious positions, consider the author of the Acts of the Apostles, who portrayed Peter and his followers as still considering the temple as integral to their piety (Acts 3:1, 5:12, 42). Stephen, however, was portrayed by that same author as preaching that Christians who still worship at the temple were resisting the Holy Spirit (Acts 7:48-51). One faith here supports two conflicting religious beliefs right within the New Testament itself. Ibid., 137.

a humble but a considered opinion. If the choice were merely arbitrary, there would be no rational consideration at all. An arbitrary decision could be reached by the flip of a coin. Even though rational people may disagree, they may not be merely arbitrary about the outcome and still be rational.

The situation is analogous to a trial by jury in American jurisprudence. After all the pertinent facts and arguments have been presented, the issue should be submitted to the jury only if, in the judge's opinion, reasonable people could disagree on the verdict. If reasonable people could not disagree, the judge should then bypass the jury by granting a motion for a directed verdict. In certain issues, such as the historicity of the Lazarus account, reasonable, faithful people may, and do in fact, disagree. Both sides can lay claim to being rational, and both can lay claim to being faithful.[45] They are united in faith because, in this instance, they are united in the meaning of the passage. They agree that there is an epiphany of the divine for those who catch on to the gist of the story. The core of faith, the way they assemble experiences and images of life, would seem to be close enough to call them partners in faith.

If faith were too caught up in philosophical jargon, one wonders how many people could have (or would want to have) faith. As imagination, faith offers itself as an environment for living human life to the fullest. In that case, even the simple-minded may have an authentic faith. Faith as imagination, therefore, can be viewed as that which connects people to their God in a way that bestows a certain richness in living.

C. Pastoral Contributions

William Lynch's contributions to theological insight have been profound in both method and content. Yet those insights would amount to little if they did not affect the pastoral life of the Church.

---

45. We ought not overlook other possibilities, equally capable of being argued rationally as the two extremes discussed above, namely, that we as faithful Christians simply do not know whether the Lazarus passage is historically accurate or not. We should not dismiss the possibility that the story contains some sort of historical core that was subsequently embellished.

It is important, therefore, to list some of the practical implications of Lynch's theology.

First, recognizing the significance of images as the meeting ground of people with one another and with their God, pastors ought to attend diligently to the images they display in homilies, catechetics, liturgy, architecture, etc. Although the ability to articulate sound doctrine is important, those teachings risk a lack of credibility if they are unaccompanied by pertinent images. Images are not mere "attention getters" in homilies. Images speak, think, and feel. They motivate us to act. Images ought to be selected with that in mind. Even the architecture of the church building with its use of space, statues, vigil lights, and altar suggest a certain way of speaking, thinking, feeling, and acting. They invite a certain sort of approach to God. They embody the sensibility of the faith.

Second, those who attempt to convert people in the modern world need to realize that they do not confront a people without faith in order to persuade them to adopt a faith. Any sane person has a faith, a way of putting together facts so that they make sense. Some of those secular images are true in the best Christian sense of the word, while other images may well nurture division, hatred, and self-absorption. It is too simple to inveigh against all "secular" images. More effective evangelization can occur with an inspection of secular images and in an illustration of how some of those images may be compromised by other conflicting images. Advances may be attained by new images of the secular, ones that take secularity seriously, on its own terms. A Christian need not feel inferior at having to justify the existence of faith in a person's life. Everyone has a faith. Sometimes it is examined, and sometimes it is not. Evangelization can be the occasion of the examination of a person's prereflective faith, with an invitation to adopt an ironic Christian imagination that puts us in touch with the divine through the human.

Third, since the divine "One" is found in the "many" of creation, Christians should realize that attempted spiritual flights away from this world simply remove them from God. That is not to say that periodic retreats and introspective soul-searching are bad. Quite the opposite. They are sorely needed, especially given the hustle and bustle of the modern world. The point is that it would be a mistake to seek our salvation there. Salvation is not found in flight from this world, but in involvement with it in such a way that the divine can emerge through human recognition and response. Flight from the world is flight from God. Therefore, the faithful ought to seek a broad insertion into their local cultures, as Lynch recommends, not only to evangelize but also to help sustain their act of faith. The broader the insertion the better. The arts, theology, philosophy, science, and other cultural pursuits should contribute each in its own way to the life of faith.

Fourth, beliefs should not be seen on the same level as faith. Beliefs are less basic, and more shifting than faith. One faith can support several analogous beliefs. Hence, a pastoral sensitivity needs to be exercised with respect to the relativity of belief that properly attaches to various scriptural and magisterial texts. All beliefs are proposed from a viewpoint and are therefore relative. For example, the story of Noah's ark ought to lead us to reflect on the gratuity of God's wish for peace with humanity. As the ancient Babylonian texts reveal, our God need not have treated us with such concern.[46] Instead, if the presentation of the passage leads to an engrossing discussion of the whereabouts of Noah's ark today, then the relativity of belief has run amok. Similarly, magisterial documents written in Scholastic terms need to be interpreted with an awareness of the limitations of that philosophical system, as well as of the historical context of the times in which they were proposed. Documents such as *Pascendi* and the Oath against Modernism need to be seen in that light.

Fifth, since we meet each other in our images, there needs to be a good deal of care in the way various groups in the Church are imagined. How might we keep the positive aspects of the image of "pastor" from becoming a dead metaphor while avoiding

---

46. Catholic exegete Bruce Vawter has noted that "in the Mesopotamian stories of the flood no real motivation is ever offered to explain why the gods brought about this particular disaster, not even in the legend of Atra-hasis. . . . What the bible has done is to turn an amoral myth into a highly moral parable of God's retribution and grace responding to the challenge of his creatures' willfulness and evil-doing." Bruce Vawter, *On Genesis: A New Reading* (Garden City N.Y.: Doubleday, 1977), 116.

inadequate images of the laity? What is an appropriate image of the laity as they exist in today's world? What images can be found to express creatively the frustration of groups that suffer discrimination in the Church? Too often highly emotional words construct barriers rather than bridges to insight and reconciliation. Images possess enormous power. They lie at the root of our conceptual structures. They are the vehicles of worship. They need to be treated cautiously.

Sixth, because images form the vehicle of our worship, there ought to be a renewed emphasis on the sacramental life of the Church. The sacramental signs that are placed in worship require more than a univocal imagination that sees only the surface. The objective sign of the sacrament symbolized by the *ex opere operato* doctrine is meaningless by itself. The objective cannot exist without the subjective. Signs are posited in the objective order only in the hopes that someone will be present who can meaningfully deal with those signs. An emphasis on the subjective *ex opere operantis* aspect of sacraments needs much attention in terms of the imagination that binds the two together. The univocal imagination can barely get beyond the fact that "bread is bread is bread," or that the Body of Christ on the cross is the body of Christ risen is the Body of Christ in the Eucharist is the Body of Christ the Church. For the univocal imagination, they are all the same. This predicament can cause countless difficulties, such as the scrupulosity that arises from a physicalist treatment of the Eucharist. The analogical imagination perceives the same and the different in proper proportion in the sacramental sign. By the fact that the sign is placed "in the Holy Spirit" in a way that is expressive of the life of Jesus, the faithful can discern the real presence of the Risen Christ in terms other than the physicalist notions of a misplaced piety of former days. That same type of analogical imagination needs to be brought to bear on all the sacraments.

Finally, the real-life stories of people, together with the images that emerge from those stories, as supplemented by the images of the classics, ought to be heard by the Church leaders. Without our stories, we do not really know who we are. Each story is a tale of love, freedom, and commitment as it has met the diffraction of this world. Each story tells us something of the human and therefore something of the divine as well. To be a community, we need to have a common poetic meaning and common values, which imply a common story. It needs to be heard in the concrete, even if only at retreats, days of recollection, in spiritual direction, or in the confessional. Penitential practices, if they are to be effective at all, need to touch on those relevant images that can heal or reconcile the story that has broken from the common meaning of the people of God. Relevant images can be determined in part by the stage of faith we have attained. The standard penance of the standard prayers for the standard sins is the product of a standard ritual that saves no one. If it is true that we meet each other and our God through images, then those images can be used wisely in the sacrament of penance – where people are most open, most vulnerable, and most able to accept and integrate a healing image in their lives. It is in penance particularly that we can give affectionate images to human frailty that is all too often denied through acts of sin.[47]

The list could go on. The world of the imagination as it comes to expression through the world of art contains profound resources not only for theology but also for the pastoral practice of the Church's ministers. The way in which each Christian uses the world of images is itself an act of the imagination. There are no rules governing how each is to bring that gift before God's people. The only rule is the nonrule of St. Augustine to love and do what you will.

---

47. Although some people find it too difficult to pray in images, many can profit from the prayerful contemplation of an image. For example, a penitent's sins may stem from a poor self-image. A reasonable penance might include a prayer of active imagination in which a person is asked to visualize a room in which he or she is seated and sees many acquaintances, each of whom pays little or no attention to the penitant. Instead of feeling angry or depressed, the penitent is to imagine Jesus walking into the room, sitting beside the person, and hugging the penitent. He or she ought to imagine Jesus explaining how much he loves not just humanity in general, but him or her in particular. Then the penitent tells Jesus about hurts, sorrows, pains, etc., and pictures Jesus' love. Obviously the scene is a fantasy on one level, but on a deeper level it is an image of God's love for each individual. Hopefully, the penance could begin to restore the penitent's self-image and could begin to erode a root of sinfulness in the person's life.

V. A Theological Pitch Pipe

It would be difficult to deny that believers are dreamers and visionaries of sorts. Life without dreams and visions would be stark and ultimately less real than the life that is enriched by the dreams of the faithful. It is by virtue of such dreams that we can begin to see into reality and to have any hope of "seeing" the unseeable God at all. But to do that we need to be able to keep our heads. We need to be able to sing the psalms in tune with a pitch pipe that will allow a rationally calibrated scale to make its contribution. Only then can we listen to a music that is moving – a music that moves us into reality and does not drown out all thought, as with the hapless Ichabod Crane.

William Lynch's thought on the imagination illustrates how the task of imagining the real is foundational to any theological effort. Facts cannot be taken for granted. They are never "pure." They are always a part of a greater imaginative framework that colors any subsequent rational analysis. The way we imagine something constitutes the faith we have about that topic. The way facts are taken in and put together, the whole that they form, the dynamics that they display are all present in the imagination. Reason then unfolds those hidden elements and relations, offering a critique as it encounters faith's beliefs and practices. But even that critique takes place in terms of an imagination. Of course the problem is that the imagination can be arbitrary, can disregard all limits, and can fall into Prometheanism. It might disregard the rational by becoming Dionysian, or it might disregard the affective and become Apollonian. Lynch was well aware of the pitfalls of the imagination. All the more reason to tend to the operation of the imagination, not suppress it. All the more reason to explore the benefits of the ironic Christic imagination so we might be led to a fruitful encounter with the personal facts of our lives as they are lived in relation to the divine.

Faith is reasonable, but it is not exhausted in reason. It is a horseman riding the steed of affective life, but it is not a headless horseman. Faith is not blind. It loves and therefore can see what others cannot. Furthermore, faith has eyes that can unify the person and the world. If Ichabod Crane were truly faithful, not merely credulous, then he would not bring a shrewd, rational, cold self to the schoolhouse by day, and an affable, simple-minded dupe to the forest at night. Instead, he would bring a unity of sensibility to both endeavors: a love that can reason and a reason that can love. We must trust to use the eyes of faith. Those eyes show us our task in life: to love in such a way that we make room for the diffraction of reality and the irony of faith. In that way, perhaps, we can maintain the courage to remain faithful to the end.

APPENDIX I

The Imagination

THE IMAGINATION WAS POSITIVELY DISTRUSTED BY THE SCHOLASTICS. Some Modernists referred to the imagination, but they did not seem to develop its potential. William Lynch placed the workings of the imagination at the very center of his theology. Of course, Lynch was not the first to explore the workings of the imagination as it relates to faith and knowledge.[1] With the exception of John Henry Newman, those who explored the role of the imagination were not Catholic, a circumstance that could serve only to increase Catholic suspicions.

Although Hume had already proposed the rather common view that the imagination harbors only a faint impression of reality, Kant elaborated more profound functions that the imagination performs. First, the reproductive imagination starts with sensory data, and gathers and organizes them. Memory is one of the common functions of the reproductive imagination. It became apparent to Kant that the organizing function of imagination is not simply reproductive. There is a "transcendental imagination" at work that organizes the a prioris into a universal system that necessarily informs all experience. It constitutes a preestablished ordering principle for the imagination, and its consideration led

---

1. For an example of the Scholastic distrust of the imagination, see Louis Billot, *De Immutabilitate Traditionis*, 84. For examples of the modernist handling of the concept of imagination, see George Tyrrell, *Faith of Millions*, 239; and Friederich von Hügel, *Essays and Addresses*, 115. A useful history of thought on the religious imagination is contained in several essays in James Mackey, *Religious Imagination* (Edinburgh: Edinburgh University Press, 1986).

Kant to investigate the effect of imagination on experience. It follows that there is a "productive imagination" that takes the a prioris and imposes order onto experience. The productive imagination molds experience according to a point of view. This happens through schemata that are used in connecting a concept with an image. The schemata are patterns by which sensory data make sense to a person. For example, Arabic numerals become imagined symbols for quantities, even though they bear no apparent relation to an actual quantity. Language constitutes another type of schema by which sensory experience becomes organized. The very "nature" of something that is perceived is also the result of this productive imagination. When theologians speak of the nature of God, reachable only as a conclusion from the practical reason, it too results from the productive imagination.[2]

On the other hand, for Hegel, revelation of the Absolute Idea comes to manifestation first through the imagination (*Vorstellung*), and it becomes expressed in art. But art is the lowest, the most vulgar, of manifestations because sensual symbols are used. Religion, as it begins to employ intellectual symbols or inadequate concepts, reaches a higher plane. It constitutes an initial breaking away from vulgar imagination, but it remains inadequate and impure.

The God of Philosophy is manifested through the *Begriff*, or the adequate concept. The concept is adequate because it is purely intellectual. Not that Hegel would rid the world of the arts and imagination. Far from it. They can be inspiring to all. They merely need to be kept in their place, since they have been sublated by the adequate concept in philosophy.[3]

A. Friederich Schelling

Friederich Schelling, a younger contemporary of Hegel, proposed a more positive role for the imagination. In Schelling's thought,

---

2. James Engell, *The Creative Imagination: Enlightenment to Romanticism* (Cambridge: Harvard University Press, 1981), 128-33.

3. Karl Löwith, *From Hegel to Nietzsche: The Revolution in Nineteenth Century Thought*, trans. D. Green (Garden City: Doubleday, 1967), 328-29.

German Idealism seems to show most clearly its potential for unlocking the riches of the imagination in relation to faith.[4]

As an idealist, Schelling proposed that each concrete element of creation tends to give expression to a continually unfolding idea. As such, the evolving world of nature gives concrete expression to God's imagination. For Schelling, the subjective impulses of the *ich bin* (I am) meet the objective forces of the *es gibt* ("there is," but also "it gives") of nature, and are resolved in the piece of art. Imagination, *Einbildungskraft*, resolves that duality in a symbol. Far from being a mere flight into a dream world, art contributes objectively to knowledge.[5]

Schelling recognized three powers or levels of imaginative activity in people. There is a passive imagination (*ursprüngliche Anschauung*) that receives sense impressions, an active component (*Einbildungskraft*) that orders those impressions into a meaningful whole, and a creative or artistic imagination (*Kunstvermögen* or *Dichtungsvermögen*) through which a person's dialectic with nature is brought to expression. As that subjective-objective duality is resolved through the work of the creative imagination expressed in works of art, self-consciousness is attained. Art is for humanity what nature is for God. Imagination frees a person from subjectivity by the creation of art whereby the self becomes objectified, real, and in relation to concrete reality. Imagination liberates the person from the confines of the self. Through acts of the creative imagination, a person becomes real. Through the mediating power of imagination, reality is attained. It is there that a person "imitates" God, or participates in the divine, most closely.[6]

Because imagination is the power through which a person escapes from the self and becomes actively related to the world, Schelling sees imagination as a form of love. Anything less involves a failure, an impoverishment, of the imagination. Thus,

---

4. Engell, *Creative Imagination*, 301-21.

5. Friederich Schelling, *Sämmtliche Werke*, ed. K. Schelling, vol. 3, *System des transcendentalen Idealismus* (Stuttgart: J. G. Cotta'Scher Verlag, 1858), 344, 392-94, 432-54.

6. Engel, *Creative Imagination*, 624-28, 610-11, 607, 615, 621-22, 613-18.

imagination bears all the freedom, as well as all the responsibility, of love.[7]

B. Samuel Taylor Coleridge

Samuel Taylor Coleridge's thought on the imagination is of interest because he brought together the thought of so many different thinkers. As an idealist, he relies particularly on Schelling. While there is much material on the imagination in Coleridge's thought, it is somewhat disorganized and, at times, inconsistent.[8]

Coleridge contended that the imagination is a faculty that freely moves about the other faculties and adapts itself to the characteristics of those faculties so that it might receive suitable impressions that can be translated or rendered intelligible to other faculties through images. In that way, reason becomes diffuse throughout a person's being, and information from the lower faculties can be transmitted to the higher. Consequently, the imagination unifies the processes of the mind and the heart. That ability to produce a mutually effective interpenetration of the faculties is the "esemplastic" power of the imagination.[9]

The imagination not only performs that esemplastic function, but it also reflects the spirit that unfolds in nature. The same God who established the laws of nature placed the human person in nature. Just as there is a unifying imaginative function within the human mind, so too there is an imagination that provides the same dynamism for nature. Imagination is a godlike power that offers a "unified perspective" on spirit, existence, and matter. Hence, art, as the product of imagination, not only can copy nature, it can imitate nature. Through the imagination, a person may be said to participate in the divine activity in the world. Religion is one expression of a person's union with the divine

---

7. Ibid., 601-4.
8. See Engel, *Creative Imagination*, 328, 328-66; Mary Warnock, *Imagination* (Berkeley: University of California Press, 1976), part 3.
9. Samuel Taylor Coleridge, *The Collected Works of Samuel Taylor Coleridge*, ed. K. Coburn, vol. 7, *Biographia Literaria*, vol. 1, ed. J. Engell and W. Bate (Princeton: Princeton University Press, 1983): 168-70, 295-300; vol. 2: 18, 167. See Engel, *Creative Imagination*, 339.

through the symbolic power of the imagination. As such, the aesthetic imagination has epistemological value because art is not primarily "self-expression," but a sort of self-identification with another. That activity not only enhances the self, it constitutes a sort of report on a reality that has come in touch with the human.[10]

The secondary imagination is sensitive to the conscience within the poet. Ultimately that moral sense cannot be proven. It is a matter of faith. The artistic imagination does not create the moral life. If it did, art would be "moralistic" in the worst sense. Rather, the imagination gives expression to what lies deepest within the human: the spiritual life of will and reason as they strike a harmony with universal reason and the absolute will of God. The imagination, at its most profound, seeks to give expression to that harmony with God.[11]

Coleridge attempted to explain our relationship with God through the dialectic that is established with the Trinity through the Son. The Son functions as the imagination of God. Christ may be seen as the "esemplastic" power of God, the power that receives from the divine and transforms the contents so that what is received may be congenially transmitted to others. Conversely, Christ is in the position of receiving from creation, and, by virtue of his esemplastic function, translating the contents to God. A mutual change is effected as the human becomes more deeply part of the divine, and the divine becomes more deeply part of the human. The interpenetrating function of the imagination, performed for man and God through Christ, thus achieves a union between God and the human.[12]

---

10. Coleridge, *Biographia Literaria*, 1: 156, 241-42, 252, 285-86; 2: 16-17, 150. See Engel, *Creative Imagination*, 349, 355.

11. Coleridge, *Biographia Literaria*, 1: 114, 202-3, 135; *The Complete Works of Samuel Taylor Coleridge*, vol. 5, *The Literary Remains; Confessions of an Inquiring Spirit*, ed. W. Shedd, (New York: Harper and Brothers, 1884), 564-65.

12. Samuel Taylor Coleridge, "Formula Fidei de Sanctissima Trinitate," *Complete Works*, vol. 5, 18-19; *Complete Works*, vol. 1, *Aids to Reflection*, 246; Engel, *Creative Imagination*, 365.

The "Eight Hypotheses" of Plato's Parmenides

THE FOLLOWING BRIEF SUMMARY IS INTENDED TO GIVE SOME IDEA OF the complexity of the Platonic logic as Lynch developed it in his commentary, *An Approach to the Metaphysics of Plato through the Parmenides of Plato* (1959), the short synopsis given in his book, *The Integrating Mind: An Exploration into Western Thought* (1962).[1] The fundamental problem of the dialogue is the reconciliation of contraries such as relative being and relative nonbeing.

Parmenides confronted this problem univocally. Being could mean only one thing: *either* something is *or* it is not. It is as simple as that. Only being is. There is no such thing as nonbeing. This common-sense view, however, could not adequately account for change (where something becomes what it was not), nor could it account for the validity of negative judgments (where it is affirmed that there is some quality of nonbeing to a thing – such as the affirmation that this "horse is not white"); nor could it account for plurality (if beings were merely a monotonous one, how could there be a many?). The statements of Parmenides that seemed so obvious failed to explain those equally obvious experiences of everyday life.[2]

Lynch notes that the neo-Parmenidean Atomists recognized those difficulties, and saw the need to posit in some way the

---

1. There is also a somewhat truncated summary given in *CA* 140-52.

2. *CA* 142-43.

"existence" of nonbeing. Their solution was to claim that all reality is comprised of particles that are separated from each other. The open space between the particles was simply nonbeing. Change could be explained by the fact that the particles could be reassembled differently. The atoms are pure being, and the nonbeing is only mixed with the beings. But the relationship between each atom and the space around it is the same as proposed by Parmenides. Each being was an entity unto itself, having only a purely external relationship with other beings.[3]

Lynch notes that Plato, turned away from his early doctrine of Ideas in *The Republic*, and achieved a more satisfying and a much more complex system to explain the metaphysical structure of finite entities in his mature works. In *The Parmenides*, Plato sought to describe a relationship between being and nonbeing that went beyond the limitations of Parmenides' univocal considerations. In this dialogue, Plato does not concern himself with absolute being and absolute nonbeing. In an absolute sense, they are contradictories. Either being is or it is not. However, when finite beings are considered, the situation becomes more complex. Lynch notes that change can occur because a finite being does not exhaust the notion of being, but it is only a relative being. As such, it is mixed with relative non being as its contrary. Relative being and relative nonbeing do not exist outside of each other in finite things as the Atomists proposed, rather, they are contraries that reside right within the heart of any entity. Relative nonbeing is that which accounts for the fact that any particular being has limits, that it is this thing and not that thing. For example, relative nonbeing accounts for the fact that *this* mouse is not *that* mouse. It helps Plato account for plurality. The one and the many not only *can* be found together, they can *only* be found together. The one is not found outside of the many, nor the many outside of the one. Nor are they found bound together by some third term.[4]

Plato guides the reader to this conclusion exploring the one and the many as contraries. What is true for the one and the many

---

3. *CA* 143.
4. *CA* 149.

will be true for any pair of contraries. By the "one," Lynch contended that Plato meant any "one," any "unit," any finite entity. Synonyms for "the many" include "the other," the "infinite," the "unlimited," and the "indeterminate."[5]

In grappling with the problem of the unification of opposites, Plato became ruthlessly logical. The solution could not, however, be offered in one definitive statement. Instead, Plato proposed the "eight hypotheses" that treat separate aspects of the problem sequentially. Only after all eight hypotheses have been treated together can the unification of opposites be seen as logical and even necessary. Lynch admitted that at times Plato seemed to be playing word games, but if his complicated logic is pursued to the end, a profound system will emerge to handle the unification of opposites. At times, a hypotheses will focus on only one contrary as if it could exist on its own – as if the right could exist without the left. Plato's reasoning process merely draws out the incoherence of such a position. Using the one and the many as a paradigm for all fundamental contraries, Plato proposes the following eight hypotheses.

Hypothesis I: Wherever there is a true, absolute one, then all predication of it is impossible.

In order to affix a predicate to anything, a duality of some sort would need to be introduced. Thus even the predication, "the one is identical to itself," creates a slight sort of duality that necessarily compromises the notion of absolute oneness. Even the statement "the one exists" implies a divisibility between oneness and existence, a duality that the "one" strictly speaking cannot tolerate. Hence, to the extent anything is simply "one" and not "many," it cannot even be said to exist.[6]

---

5. When Lynch associates the one with the finite and the many with infinity, he is treating *finite or composed* entities only. The notion of God's infinity is used in a very different way. God's infinity is associated with mystery.

6. William F. Lynch, *An Approach to the Metaphysics of Plato through the Parmenides* (Washington, D.C.: Georgetown University Press, 1959), 50-51. Hereinafter cited as "*PP.*"

This hypothesis might be related to a musical analogy in the following way: given the fact that a symphony has been played (given the fact that creation exists), there are no monolithic, "one-note" symphonies.

Hypothesis II: Every one is a Whole composed of principles of unity and multiplicity.

Plato now presents the one, not as a strict absolute one, but as a "whole" that consists of parts or members that it unifies. This hypothesis is not a rejection of the first hypothesis. There is still a sense in which, to the extent that anything is "one," it is indivisible. Yet experience tells us that any finite one is composed of parts. There is something about a "one" that is indivisible (once divided, it loses its status as a one), and yet divisible (the parts of a whole can be subdivided infinitely but are still limited by their membership in the whole). Thus, contraries can be present within an entity at the same time. Here we see also that it is not true to speak of *a* one *and a* many, *a* limited *and an* unlimited, or any other pairs of contraries in a disjunctive sort of way. The two are not juxtaposed, or bonded by any intervening principle. They are predicated of the same entity. The one is *both* one *and* many. The many are not coabsolute with the one. They exist only by virtue of their participation in the one.[7]

Considering the analogy of music, Plato here is merely saying that a symphony is a unity of parts, it is a whole. There are identifiable notes that make up the whole of the symphony.

Hypothesis IIa: There is a point of transition in time between two contraries (found in moments of change and becoming) that cannot be measured in time and cannot be characterized in terms of either of the contraries.

Just as it is possible to predicate *both* contraries to a one (Hypothesis 2), so too there are circumstances in which it is possible that neither contrary will do: neither one nor many, neither being nor

---

7. *PP* 100, 120-21, 98-99, 101.

nonbeing, etc. Examples of this involve change and becoming. It can be seen in events of combination, separation, motion, coming to rest, and appearance or disappearance in being. Plato here is concerned with the so-called instant. It consists of that moment precisely between the object as resting and the object as moving. That point in between cannot be calculated solely in terms of either rest or motion. Parmenides would say that being is, nonbeing is not, and there is nothing between them. Plato would say that being is, but not in the absolute sense of Hypothesis 1; that nonbeing is, but not in the absolute sense of Hypothesis 1; and that the "instant" is, but, again, not in the absolute sense of Hypothesis 1. Here we have a positive form of nonbeing located right in the heart of being.[8]

In terms of a musical analogy, one might observe that a symphony has parts that move, that change. Therefore, there are times in its performance that are bereft of any contraries. As violin music ascends the scale from E to F, there is an instant in which the tone is neither E nor F. Neither "contrary" will do. It also happens between interludes of sound and silence.

Hypothesis III: The parts exist as parts only by virtue of the one.

The parts share in the whole, and gain their identity from the whole. Of themselves, the parts are simply a "sheer many," and even a pure infinite. The parts, even though infinitely divisible, derive their definiteness from the one. Previously, Plato had shown the co-presence of contraries. Here he defines their relationship. The one dominates the many, and gives them their being.[9]

Here Plato is saying that any note in the symphony gains its meaning, its identity, from the greater sweep of music that surrounds that note. The principle of unity comes from the symphony as a whole, not from the individual notes.

---

8. *PP* 183, 140, 142, 143-44. Id., *The Integrating Mind: An Exploration into Western Thought* (New York: Sheed and Ward, 1962), 168. Hereinafter cited as "*IM*."
9. *PP* 148, 158.

Hypothesis IV: Even though the one is made up of the many,
the many are different from the one.

Plato now states that the "unlimited" is different from the "one."
Only the one is one. The "others," the members, contribute nothing
to the oneness, though oneness in a sense may be communicated
to them by virtue of the one in which they participate. Now Plato
is in a position to deny all contraries in the Platonic many. The
many now take on the aspect of the "indeterminate." For example,
if others are not one, then neither are they many. After all, units
are needed to establish the many. The many without the one is
so indefinite that this "sheer many" can no longer be said to exist.
Furthermore, if there is no unity, then the contraries "like-unlike"
cannot exist since a "like" implies a unity and an "unlike" implies
at least two units. Therefore, if any of those contraries exist, a
"one" must exist. That "one" alone specifies a thing to be what it
is both in its aspect as unity, and in its multiple aspect. Hence, the
unity that was so problematic in Hypothesis 1 is now restored.[10]

Extending the analogy from music, Plato is saying that a
concert is not just an accumulation of notes. It needs a plan, an
idea, a schema, a tune, that stands outside of the individual notes
to organize them into a pleasing unity. There is no tune without
the notes, but the notes do not produce the tune. The composer
does.

Hypothesis V: The one is limited in relation to the rest of the
real because of the presence of otherness, or difference, or rela-
tive nonbeing.

It is a matter of common experience that there is more than one
"one." How can that logically be? Within the interior structure of
each one, there is an element of nonbeing that "prevents it from
exhausting the whole range of oneness." It is that element of
nonbeing (not being the other) that allows multiplicity to emerge.
Significantly, Lynch notes that throughout the eight hypotheses,
Plato will either use both terms of a contrary in relation to an entity

---

10. *PP* 176, 166; *IM* 170.

or neither. Contraries are always found together, or they are not found at all. It would be incoherent to describe an entity simply as a "one" while attempting to exclude the "many," or the "other."[11]

In terms of a musical analogy, Plato is saying that a composer can create more than one symphony, or perhaps that there can be identifiable parts to a symphony that can be pleasing and meaningful in themselves. Thus, movements to symphonies can themselves be pleasant music even though heard out of their greater context.

Hypothesis VI: If a one is not, then it does not exist, and nothing can be said of it, and it cannot be the object of thought.

Plato here takes up the Parmenidean concept of absolute nonbeing. If a one is not, then nothing can be said of it. It simply does not exist, and, unlike relative nonbeing, it has absolutely no relation to being. None of the contraries can describe it. It is interesting here that not even nonbeing as a contrary could describe this absolute nonexistent.[12]

At the symphonic level, if one were to claim that only silence existed, there could be no music. Silence makes sense only as relative to sound. One could not claim that silence simply exists. So does the sound of music. In fact, music often makes good use of silence. Both share a relative, not an absolute, existence.

Hypothesis VII: It is possible to attempt to view the whole without grasping its principle of unity. The result is the mere appearance of unity.

Plato next considers *doxa* (appearance), or the faculty that is midway between knowledge and ignorance. The object of *doxa* is the world of becoming because it is midway between being and nonbeing. In this world of curbstone opinions, people tend to want to keep unity and multiplicity on the same plane. They

---

11. *PP* 187-88; *IM* 172.
12. *PP* 203-4.

attempt to hold together all the parts without the principle of unity. This results in an illegitimate confusion of contraries. Plato is not proposing that the one *is the same as* the many, nor is he proposing a mere juxtaposition of the one and the many. Rather, he proposes a one through the many, and a many through the one.[13]

At the musical level, one might imagine the notes of a symphony becoming scrambled. Even though the same notes are present, the principle of unity is lost. For example, if someone took the notes of the "Rhapsody in Blue" and rearranged them alphabetically, the result would not be an arrangement of "Rhapsody in Blue" even though the same notes were present. The overarching perspective would be lost. If there were any chance resemblance to the original, it would be mere *doxa,* mere appearance.

Hypothesis VIII: Here Plato states that, in spite of Hypothesis 1 (where it was concluded that it could not be said that the one exists all by itself), if there is no principle of one, then the "many" do not exist.

Logically, for there to be a many, there must be more than one "one." If that is impossible, then nothing exists.[14]

At the musical level, we might say here that if the very notion of having even one sound does not exist, then the notion of having many sounds does not exist.

Presenting all eight hypotheses together, Plato thus proposed that finite being is a complex tensive reality that "leaves room for" relative nonbeing. Plato employs a doctrine of double participation to incorporate these insights into his metaphysics. The Platonic notion of participation operates at its first level wherever there is an identifiable "one." The members participate in the unity of that given entity. For Parmenides, there could be only a single "one": the cosmos. For Plato, there is a "one" present in every existent. Every member of that one exists only by virtue of its participation in that "one" that determines its parts. But, of

---

13. Ibid., 213, 216, 221; *IM* 174–75.
14. *PP* 231–32.

course, that one does not exhaust being. Because it also contains relative nonbeing, other "ones" are also possible.[15]

There is a second level of participation by virtue of which that limited "one" exists. A limited "one" exists according to a mode of participation in being. It shares in the being of the Idea that gives it its form. Lynch is convinced that the Platonic doctrine of Ideas teaches that each essence has meaning in itself, which does not have to look outside of itself to make sense. As things participate in more expansive Ideas, as we move from species up to genuses, to families, etc., a more sweeping unity among things may be perceived. Ultimately, all "ones" participate in the "one" Being by virtue of which they exist. So at last Plato can say with Aristotle that two things can become one only if they were never two in the first place.[16]

---

15. *PP* 241-42.
16. *PP* 243-44; *IM* 176-77.

BIBLIOGRAPHY

Works by William F. Lynch, S.J.

A. Books

An Approach to the Metaphysics of Plato through the Parmemnides.
Washington: Georgetown University Press, 1959.
The Image Industries. New York: Sheed and Ward, 1959.
Christ and Apollo: The Dimensions of the Literary Imagination.
Notre Dame: University of Notre Dame Press, 1960.
The Integrating Mind: An Exploration into Western Thought. New
York: Sheed and Ward, 1962.
Images of Hope: Imagination as Healer of the Hopeless. Notre
Dame: University of Notre Dame Press, 1965.
Christ and Prometheus: A New Image of the Secular. Notre Dame:
University of Notre Dame Press, 1970.
Images of Faith: An Exploration of the Ironic Imagination. Notre
Dame: University of Notre Dame Press, 1973.

B. Unpublished Manuscripts

A Book of Admiration, undated.
Drama of the Mind, undated.

C. Articles

"Plato and the Absolute State." *The Modern Schoolman: A Quarterly Journal of Philosophy* 16, no. 1 (November 1938): 14-17.
"Art and the Objective Mind." *Jesuit Education Quarterly* 2, no.
2 (1939): 78-82.

"Of Rhythm and Its End." *Spirit: A Magazine of Poetry* 6, no. 5 (November 1939): 148-51. Also in *Return to Poetry: Critical Essays from Spirit.* Edited by J.G. Brumini et al., 85-88. New York: Declan X. McMillan, 1947.

"Value of the Arts as Inspirer of Poet and Saint." *America* 62 (December 30, 1939): 327-28.

"The Meaning of Mud." *Spirit: A Magazine of Poetry* 6, no. 6 (January 1940): 178-85.

"Bringing the Furies to Fordham." *America* 47, no. 1 (April 11, 1942): 45-46.

"Can the Church Revive the Drama?" *America* 67, no. 21 (August 29, 1942): 577-78.

"On the Catholic Word." *America* 70 (November 6, 1943): 129-30.

"Liturgy and Theatre." *Liturgical Arts,* 12 (November 1943): 3-10.

"A Play." *Messenger of the Sacred Heart* 83, no. 2 (February 1948): 52-53.

"The Sacrament of Our Times." *Messenger of the Sacred Heart* 83, no. 3 (March 1948): 56-61.

"We Must Make Reparation." *Messenger of the Sacred Heart* 83, no. 5 (May 1948): 66-70.

"Your Family and the Sacred Heart." *Messenger of the Sacred Heart* 83, no. 6 (June 1948): 52.

"A Message for the Alcoholic." *Messenger of the Sacred Heart* 83, no. 7 (July 1948): 39.

"A Return to Real Christianity." *Messenger of the Sacred Heart* 83, no. 8 (August 1948): 11-15.

"The Sacred Heart and Catholic Action." *Messenger of the Sacred Heart* 83, no. 9 (September 1948): 48-51.

"The Fight against Atheism." *Messenger of the Sacred Heart* 84, no. 2 (February 1949): 11-13.

"All Roads Lead to Rome." *Messenger of the Sacred Heart* 84, no. 3 (March 1949): 30-35.

"Culture and Belief." *Thought* 25, no. 98 (September 1950): 441-63.

"The Partisan Review Symposium." *Thought* 25, no. 99 (December 1950): 681-91.

"Plato: Symposium (the Banquet)." In *The Great Books: A Christian Appraisal*, vol. III. Edited by Harold Gardiner, S.J. Greenwich, CT: Devin-Adair, 1951.

"Adventure in Order." *Thought* 26, no. 100 (Winter 1951/52): 33-49.

"Confusion in Our Theatre." *Thought* 26, no. 102 (Summer 1951): 342-60.

"Mirror of the Magazines." *Thought* 26, no. 103 (December 1951): 598-605.

"Blanshardian Democracy." *Thought* 26, no. 103 (Winter 1951/52): 581-85.

"Nationalism and Internationalism." *The Catholic Mind* 52, no. 1095 (March 1954): 149-58.

"For a Redeemed Actuality." *Spirit: A Magazine of Poetry* 21. no. 1 (March 1954): 83-86.

"Theology and the Imagination." *Thought* 29, no. 112 (Spring 1954): 61-86.

"Theology and the Imagination II: The Evocative Symbol." *Thought* 29, no. 115 (December 1954): 529-554.

"Theology and the Imagination III: The Problem of Comedy." *Thought* 30, no. 116 (Spring 1955): 18-36.

"Saint Ignatius and the 'New Theological Age.' " *Thought* 31, no. 121 (Summer 1956): 187-215.

Review of *Martin Buber*, by Arthur A. Cohen. In *America* 98 (March 22, 1958): 728-29.

"The Imagination and the Finite." *Thought* 33, no. 129 (Summer 1958): 205-28

"Art and Sensibility." *Commonweal* 70 (April 10, 1959): 47-50.

"The Catholic Idea." In *The Idea of Catholicism: An Introduction to the Thought and Worship of the Church*. Edited by Walter Burghardt, 56-64. United States of America: Meridian Books, 1960.

"Ritual and Drama." *Commonweal* 71 (February 26, 1960): 586-88.

"Theology and Human Sensibility." *The Critic* 18 (April/May 1960): 15.

"The Problem of Freedom." *Cross Currents* 10 (Spring 1960): 97-114. Also in *Theology Digest* 9, no. 3 (Autumn 1961): 182-86.

"Metaphysics and the Literary Imagination." *Spirit: A Magazine of Poetry* 27, no. 5 (November 1960): 137-44.

"Let's Have Film Festivals." *America* 104, no. 23 (March 11, 1961): 753-56.

"Reality and Realism: A Distinction with a Difference." *The Critic* 20 (April-May 1962): 43-47.

"Christianity and the Passive Imagination." *The Catholic Messenger* 80 (August 30, 1962).

"The Freedom to Be Human." In *Freedom and Man.* Edited by John Courtney Murray, S.J. New York: P. J. Kennedy, 1965.

"Toward a Theology of the Secular." *Thought* 41, no. 162 (Autumn 1966): 349-65.

"Can Ministers and Psychiatrists Work Together?" *Redbook* 128 (December 1968): 52.

"A Reappraisal of Christian Symbol." *North American Liturgical Week* 28 (1967): 66-76.

"Ugliness." *New Catholic Encyclopedia.* Edited by W. J. McDonald et al., 368. New York: McGraw-Hill, 1967.

"Death as Nothingness." *Continuum* 5, no. 3 (Autumn 1967): 459-69.

"Counterrevolution in the Movies: Words, Ideas and the Artist as Thinker." *Commonweal* 87 (October 20, 1967): 77-86.

"Psychological Man." *America* 117 (November 25, 1967): 635-37.

"Commentary on Ritual and Liturgy." In *The Religious Situation.* Edited by Donald R. Cutler. Boston: Beacon, 1968.

"The Crisis of Hope." *Sister Formation Bulletin* 14 (Summer 1968): 6-10.

"Images of Faith." *Continuum* 7, no. 1 (Winter/Spring 1969): 187-94.

"Images of Faith II: The Task of Irony." *Continuum* 7, no. 3 (Autumn 1969): 478-92.

"Madness as an Existential Solution to an Existential Situation." (Review of *The Divided Self* and *Self and Others* by R. D. Laing.) *Commonweal* 92, no. 20 (September 25, 1970): 484-85.

"Faith, Experience and Imagination." *New Catholic World* 215, no. 1285 (July-August 1972): 170-73.

"In Admiration of Teilhard." *America* 132, no. 14 (April 12, 1975): 274-76.

"Euripides' 'Bacchae': The Mind in Prison." *Cross Currents* 25 (Summer 1975): 163-74.

"Advent from Head to Toe." *America* 133, no. 17 (November 29, 1975): 382-83.

"What's Wrong with 'Equus'? Ask Euripides." *America* 133, no. 19 (December 13, 1975): 419-22.

"The Imagination of the Drama." *Review of Existential Psychology and Psychiatry* 14, no. 1 (1975/1976): 1-10.

"The Task of Enlargement." *Thought* 51, no. 203 (December 1976): 345-55.

"The Psychologically Disabled." In *Human Life: Problems of Birth, of Living, and of Dying.* Pastoral Psychology Series, no. 9. Edited by William Bier. New York: Fordham University Press, 1977.

"A Dramatic Making of the Human." *Humanitas* 14, no. 2 (May 1978): 161-71.

"Foundation Stones for Collaboration between Religion and the Literary Imagination." *Journal of the American Academy of Religion* 47, no. 2, Supplement (June 1979): 329-44.

"The Drama of the Mind: An Ontology of the Imagination." *Notre Dame English Journal: A Journal of Religion in Literature* 13, no. 1 (Fall 1980): 17-28.

"The Life of Faith and Imagination: Theological Reflection in Art and Literature." *Thought* 57, no. 224 (March 1982): 7-16.

"Archtypal Theory and Spirituality." *Studies in Formative Spirituality* 4 (February 1983): 83-93.

"Me and the East River." *New York Images: A Journal of Places, Arts, Literature* 1 (Spring 1984): 3-5.

"The *Spiritual Exercises* of St. Ignatius and Their Images." *New York Images: A Journal of Places, Arts, Literature* 1 (Spring 1984): 12-13.

"Easy Dramatic Lessons on . . . How to Miss Reality, How to Hit It." *New York Images: A Journal of Places, Arts, Literature* 1, no. 1 (Spring 1984): 14-22.

"Imagining Past, Present, Future in One Piece." *Studies in Formative Spirituality* 6, no. 1 (February 1985): 65-72.

"Architecture and Theatre in Greece: The World as Actor." *New York Images: A Journal of Places, Arts, Literature* 1, no. 2 (1985): 12-15.

"Final Image: Sancho Panza and Imagination." *New York Images: A Journal of Places, Arts, Literature* 2 (1985): 28-30.

"Introduction: On the Transformation of Our Images." *New York Images: A Journal of Places, Arts, Literature* 1, no. 3 (Autumn 1986): 2-3.

"The Bacchae of Euripides: An American Parallel." *New York Images: A Journal of Places, Arts, Literature* 1, no. 3 (Autumn 1986): 20-22.

"Three Stories about . . . 1. The Cat; 2. The Dog; 3. The Dreamy Mediterranean." *New York Images: A Journal of Places, Arts, Literature* 1, no. 3 (Autumn 1986): 28-30.

Index